MEDJUGORJE
Fruits of My Promise

Medjugorje

Fruits of My Promise

CARMEL KELLY

A Marian Pilgrimage
Group Leader

columba
BOOKS

First published in 2021 by

Block 3b, Bracken Business Park,
Bracken Road, Sandyford,Dublin 18, D18 K277
www.columbabooks.com

ISBN: 978-1-78218-383-9

Set in Linux Libertine, Essones and August Script
Book and cover design by Alba Esteban | Columba Books

Cover image: Youth Festival in Medjugorje 2018
Studio: FOTO VIDEO STUDIO ĐANI © (All Rights Reserved)
Contact: https://vimeo.com/fotodjani

Printed by ScandBook, Falun

To Paul Wallace, who sadly passed away recently, David Parkes, Fr Tom, Anne Ryder, and all the pilgrims over the years who encouraged me to write down my memories.

ABOUT THE AUTHOR

Carmel Kelly was born in 1935 to Thomas and Elisabeth Butterly of 16 Marino Park, Dublin.

While pregnant with Carmel her mother developed bone cancer and had her leg amputated below the knee, which left her weak and unable to care for a newborn. Shortly after birth, Carmel was given to Elizabeth's mother and spent her first three years living in Rialto. Carmel returned to the family home after the death of her mother from TB at age 3.

Carmel's father remarried so herself and her older brother Frankie would have a mother figure growing up. She grew up in a strong Trade Union house and remembered the many visits of James Larkin as she would recount the large man with huge hands and a booming voice.

Thomas put great value in education and Carmel was a willing student who graduated from Marino college with a degree in teaching. Fluent in German, Spanish and French, Carmel loved to travel and did so throughout Europe in her early twenties – Lourdes being one of her first destinations. Her first full time job was with Sisks as a secretary. This is where she met her husband Bill in 1960. A widower with 4 children; they married in 1962 and had 2 children together.

In 1969 they emigrated to Australia where Bill worked as a steel fixer and Carmel worked as secretary to the Managing Director of Tubemakers. It was at this time she started to deal on the stock market and became very adept at making money for herself and her boss, trading in both shares and commodities.

The family finally decided to return to Ireland in 1982 and initially settled in Athboy before her stepmother's failing heath forced the move back to Dublin, where they settled in East Wall. With her enduring love of Our Lady and strong beliefs, Carmel soon became involved in the local prayer group and parish activities.

However, it was Bill's desire to visit Medjugorje, and he finally convinced her to go in June of 1997. It was not to be for Bill; he passed on the 12th of May, a short time after being diagnosed with cancer. Before he died he made Carmel promise to go for the both of them. This she did 110 times over twenty two years, bringing thousands with her.

When the lockdown came Carmel didn't rest. At the age of 85 she sat down and wrote this book telling some of the many stories of people who found peace in a small town in Bosnia: a remarkable little place called Medjugorje.

Carmel finished her book just weeks before being admitted to hospital, where on September 26th 2020 she passed from Covid-19. Our Lady called her faithful servant home, her work finished.

CONTENTS

FOREWORD

There are so many Marian shrines, including Knock in Ireland, my home country, but in the late 1990's I loved Lourdes and made sure to be there every two years. My husband Bill would not go to Lourdes so I went with friends.

Then Bill read about Medjugorje and wanted to go there. I didn't want to go to Medjugorje, but agreed to go for his sake.

We made our plans, plans never to be fulfilled, as Bill became ill. It was as a result of a promise made to him that I eventually travelled to Medjugorje. Here I tell the story of how keeping this promise, made to my husband in his last days, would change the course of my life.

I tell how the years following that first eventful journey would bring me, through the blessings of others, many, many personal blessings.

INTRODUCTION

This book is being written at the request of so many who have said 'you should write a book'. There was never time until COVID-19 came, stopping us all in our tracks. Someone rang me and said, 'Now write the book'. I am trying, and if it is the will of the Lord and his Blessed Mother, whose help I ask, I will succeed.

I do not intend, in a big way, to retell the story of what happened in Medjugorje almost 40 years ago as most people reading this book will, I believe, already know that story. I will however, touch on it more in relation to the six visionaries themselves, what they may have expected at that time and the course their lives have actually taken. This book is more about my going to Medjugorje, first in 1997, becoming a Marian Pilgrimages group leader in 1998 and about how easy this company and staff have been to work with over the years. It is about a life changing decision made in 1997 and the reason behind that decision. It is about my experiences as a group leader, people I met, stories told, lives changed and blessings received by so many – and through their blessings, the blessings I myself have been so privileged to receive. For all these years and all these blessings, I thank the Lord and his Blessed Mother, who have always sent the people needed to enable me to do this work.

Chapter One

MY STORY

I wanted to start "my story" with my Medjugorje experiences but was told this was not enough. People will ask 'who is Carmel Kelly, where does she come from, and what is her background'?

I realise this is probably true. One cannot really begin a story in the middle or near the end when only good things are happening, so I will try to give readers an insight into who I am and where I come from.

This is a story of constant faith and the grace given to me at an early age to be aware of the presence of God in my life and to know, without a shadow of doubt, that He is always there – especially in the bad times.

I was born Carmel Butterly in Dublin in 1935. My mother had a leg amputated while pregnant with me and at twenty-seven years of age was already dying of TB. I had one older brother, Frankie. Of necessity, because of my mother's illness, we lived with my father's mother, granny Butterly, and her two unmarried sons.

When I was a baby I was sent to my maternal grandmother in Rialto, granny Murray. Along with my grandfather and two aunts, I was provided with a loving environment for three years while my mother died slowly and painfully.

Living with my mother's family in Rialto for three years I had bonded with them and was settled. However, the situation changed with the death of my mother. I was taken back into the care of my father's mother in Marino. She did not have the gentle nature of my granny Murray and it was the start of a very troubled and unhappy childhood for me.

Every Saturday my granny Murray took me out for the day. My dad, who worked long hours six days a week, was off on Sundays. For me these were two good days.

My dad remarried when I was eight. It made no difference to me, as things did not improve. My new mother believed as my grandmother Butterly did and there was never a gentle touch; no sparing the rod and spoiling the child.

I went to the St Vincent De Paul school in Marino run by the French Sisters of Charity (now Daughters of Charity). I loved school, since learning was easy for me. School was better than home and I got on well with my teachers. They gave credit where it was due. There was a positive side to school. At home, in the eyes of the two women in my life, I could do no right. My brother, on the other hand, whom I loved very much, could do no wrong.

My grandmother died when I was twelve; I did not cry. I have to admit that while others mourned her passing, I felt nothing and with the honesty only a child is capable of, could not pretend otherwise, so no, I did not cry. As I had grown up I was able to tell my doctor on one occasion about the physical abuse; that abuse stopped then. I had never spoken of it to anyone, neither my father nor my granny Murray, who was still a huge part of my life and would remain so until her death in her 90's. Why do children not talk? I just know I did not!

Although my grandmother died when I was twelve, I still feared my mother until her death in 1994. My husband Bill and I moved in with her in the last years of her life when she became senile. I was quite ill at that time and could not have done it alone. Bill was my rock. I always wanted her love and approval but no matter how hard I tried I could never earn or buy it. She did love my brother, although he went to England at sixteen years of age and rarely came home. Frankie died in 1990 and I still miss him. Looking back, I know I did my best and I have no regrets.

Things improved in my early teens. I studied short-hand/typing and started work at fifteen. I took night classes in German and Spanish since I loved languages. For some reason, my faith was always strong, and I bought my first bible at fifteen years of age as I needed to know more. I was brought up with the fear of God, a God who would severely punish the smallest transgression. However, as I grew older I realised God is not this vengeful figure but a loving friend who is full of unconditional love for each and every one of us. When we distance ourselves from Him, He waits patiently for our return. I had found a faith of love and I cannot deny that in the bad times this faith has been my strength.

Between the ages of fifteen and twenty-five I worked in three different jobs, travelled to a few different countries, and still lived at home. In those days generally, young people lived at home until marriage.

My dad retired at fifty-five due to ill health and I finally developed a really close relationship with him. He listened to the stories of my workday and was very easy to talk to. He made teatimes great. I was twenty-one when he died in his sleep; he was fifty-seven. There were no more teatime conversations. My mother read the paper at teatimes and could not see me cry with loneliness for the loss of my father.

I met my future husband Bill at John Sisk, where we both worked. We married in 1962. My mother, the night before my wedding, made clear her future role in my life; no bringing my problems to her and no asking her to babysit.

We bought our first house in 1963 and the same year my first son Tony was born. I was reasonably content, although we struggled financially. When a woman married in those days, she had to leave work. Despite this I had a freedom that I never had living with my mother, as whatever I did drew criticism from her. My second son Kevin was born in 1965 and rearing those boys with love became the focus of my life.

We emigrated to Australia on the assisted passage scheme in the late sixties and remained there until the early eighties. My time in Australia played a huge part in my becoming the person I am today. Living in Ireland I was always under my mother's watchful eye. In Australia, away from this, I became really independent. I had a great job and I gained confidence. At my husband's insistence, we returned to Ireland in 1982 and I worried how my children, in their late teens and being used to the Australian lifestyle, would settle. Thankfully, they both settled and are now married with families of their own.

Returning from Australia we lived in Athboy in Co. Meath until 1990. We then moved back to Dublin and settled in East Wall. We moved to Marino in 1992 to look after my mother until she died in 1994 and remained there until after Bill's death in 1997. Having been involved with the community in East Wall since 1990 I returned there in 1998 and will remain here for the rest of my life among the wonderful and truly great friends who are always there for me when needed.

I do not tell this story out of any sense of bitterness or "getting back" at anyone for the hurts experienced. Bitterness, hatred or holding a grudge are all a waste of good energy. It would only hurt me and not the other people involved. It would be like taking poison myself and expecting others to die, so my philosophy is 'let no one rob my peace'.

I also believe those who hurt me in my childhood were a product of their generation and felt they were doing the right thing. The fact is, that was my childhood and who could say where I would be today, what kind of person I would be, had my childhood and the ensuing years not been what they were. God's gift to me was my life; my gift to Him is what I do with that life and I hope I am doing okay.

My background being told, the following account is how my life became intertwined with Medjugorje.

With both my sons married, and after my mother's death in 1994, my husband Bill and I were free agents and enjoyed the following few years of having no one to really worry about and going wherever we wanted.

A regular thing with myself and some friends was a bi-annual visit to Lourdes. This did not interest Bill, pilgrimage did not appeal to him. Little did I know how this was to change.

At that time I knew nothing about Medjugorje but someone gave me a copy of Heather Parsons book, "A Light Between the Hills" which is a series of stories of people whose lives were changed by Medjugorje. I did not read it at the time, I just left it lying around. I thought no more about it until one day in January 1997 – having read the book, Bill expressed a wish to go there. I could not know then how Bill's desire to go to Medjugorje would change my life, but I was so pleased that he wanted to go.

I finally read the book, found out about Marian Pilgrimages and booked for us to travel in April 1997. This date was subsequently changed by Marian Pilgrimages until May 22nd. This was okay with us and we were looking forward to our trip.

In March Bill was diagnosed with a bad chest infection, which after two rounds of antibiotics and steroids, showed no sign of improving. On the 15th of April our doctor sent Bill to Beaumont Hospital for an x-ray, after which he was kept in hospital for further investigation. Finally, following ten days of extensive tests, on the 25th April 1997 we were informed that Bill had extensive cancer in both lungs. Explaining our plans to the consultant, he made it clear all travel was out. Believing at that time that Bill could be treated, I explained the situation to Tom Field in Marian Pilgrimages, who could not have been nicer.

They gave us a credit note for two years and we could go when Bill was better. Telling Bill this the following day in the Hospital he asked me to promise that if he could not go to Medjugorje I would go anyway and bring my friend Agnes on his ticket. It was no use trying to explain to him that I had no interest in Medjugorje and was only going because of him, that I was quite happy with going to Lourdes every two years.

He insisted I promise to go to Medjugorje and because he was getting agitated, I made the promise, still hoping he would recover and we could go together.

We brought Bill home from hospital on the 30th of April and the team from the Hospice took over Bill's care. However, this was not to last very long as on the 12th of May 1997, seventeen days after diagnosis and ten days before our expected trip, Bill died.

The book which had prompted Bill's wish to go to Medjugorje included the story of a man called David Parkes, who in 1989, with, according to his doctors, about two weeks to live, had an instant healing of Crohn's Disease (see chapter twenty one for David's full story). One day while in Veritas in Dublin I came across his tapes. I bought his "Let Me Live" tape and brought it home. Bill and I listened for the first time to the very special voice of David Parkes. Bill was so impressed that he played the tape over and over and everyone who came to our house was made to 'Listen to this guy'. I tell this story because in Bill's last days David Parkes and this piece of music brought great comfort to him. He continued to listen to it over and over until the secondary cancers went to his brain and he could no longer communicate.

Five weeks after Bill's death and only to fulfil the promise, I explained everything to Tom Field in Marian Pilgrimages. He had no problem with my friend Agnes going to Medjugorje on Bill's ticket. So, on the 17th of June 1997, knowing nothing about the place, I set off with my friend and my daughter-in-law Marian on what was to be, 'A once off pilgrimage to Medjugorje'.

However, being invited to be present at an apparition with Ivan the Visionary on Apparition Hill at 10pm one evening, everything changed for me. In the presence of over three thousand people and standing very close to Ivan I had an unforgettable experience. Once the apparition started, the silence was total. I cried a lot, missing Bill yet feeling he was there in spirit and in my heart. I had no doubt of the presence of Our Lady at that time. I felt an incredible urge to bring others to Medjugorje and I remember saying, 'Blessed Mother, I cannot see you, I cannot hear you but I know you are here and I promise I will bring others here, but Blessed Mother I am not a salesperson - you send the people and I'll bring them'. Coming down the hill that night, Agnes could not believe when I told her what I planned, but she too has been a constant returnee with me.

Marian would return on a few occasions but more frequently in recent years. I went to Medjugorje to fulfil a promise and returned from that first visit having made another promise.

With the help of Marian Pilgrimages in May 1998 I brought my first group and two further groups in October 1998. Medjugorje took over my life. I now benefit from and am blessed by friendships made and the experiences of Medjugorje.

There is no way to explain the satisfaction and joy I derive just being with the people in my groups. Every group brings something new and every first-timer is a special blessing.

I could not have foreseen as Bill was dying, the change my life would undergo as a result of the promise made to him. This happened when all commitments were done. Family married and gone, mother and husband gone. I was a free agent and into this space came the Blessed Mother – and the rest is history!

Just as I could not know the huge part Medjugorje would play in my future life when I made the promise to Bill, neither could I realise I would come to know David Parkes personally. David eventually came to work for Marian Pilgrimages in 2001 as Pilgrim Director.

I arranged to meet him one day for lunch in Columbo's and made him aware of how his music had comforted my husband and made things easier for him in his last days. Out of this, a lasting friendship has developed.

At this stage in my life, age 85, it is still a privilege to be able to keep that promise to bring the people the Blessed Mother sends, something I could not do without her help and the help of her Son.

Chapter Two

MEDJUGORJE THE PLACE

Situated in Bosnia-Herzegovina, Medjugorje (which means "between the hills") is not very big. It is a valley nestling literally between the hills, between what is now Apparition Hill and Cross Mountain. Because of the events which took place there in 1981, it is now a very busy place with lots of souvenir shops, restaurants, guest houses, boutiques, hotels, and beauty shops - all the things associated with tourist and holiday resorts and pilgrim sites. That is Medjugorje now, but what about then, 1981? Describing the layout of Medjugorje and what it was like in 1981 is something I cannot do, as my first visit was in 1997. By then it had already changed and was continuing to change. I can only do my best, looking at old photographs and from how I found it on my first visit.

I know in 1981 the twin-spired church of St James stood alone in the valley with only the priests' house nearby. There were trees right up to the main door of the church. Directly behind the church there were vineyards and fields interspersed with trees all the way to Bijakovici and the base of Podbrdo as it was then called. There was not a single house in the valley. What is now Bosnia-Herzegovina was then part of Yugoslavia under the rule of the late Tito. Medjugorje was a place most people had never heard of. It was a tiny place with a small population mainly living around Bijakovici and the hill of Podbrdo. The people worked under the communist regime and Catholics could not openly profess their faith. To do so brought great suffering. This was the Medjugorje of 24th of June 1981 on the feast of John the Baptist. This would be the last day Medjugorje would ever be quiet. It was the day Heaven would touch earth, the day Our Lady chose to appear to six young people. From that day on this unknown village would never be the same. It is a village now known worldwide as 'a very special place'.

There is a pathway leading from near the church through the fields and vineyards to Bijakovici. The hill itself in 1981 was overgrown and used mostly by goats. After Our Lady appeared, the hill was cleared for easy access by pilgrims and Podbrdo became Apparition Hill.

Asked 'What is Medjugorje like?' I usually respond, 'Not something easily explained but something that needs to be experienced for oneself'. It is not possible to explain the sense of peace to be found there regardless of how busy it is. This is something which can only be experienced personally and the reason for that peace, I believe, is Mary's continued presence.

As a group leader I try not to push people to go to Medjugorje even when I feel it may do them good. I will talk to them about Medjugorje but if Our Lady wants them there, she will get them there; after all she got me there! If and when she invites them and they choose me as their group leader, then my job is to bring them and she will do the rest. However, I do tell all my pilgrims, 'Be aware if you go to Medjugorje once, it can become addictive'. The local people, mostly Croatians living in Bosnia-Herzegovina, are always helpful and friendly with the pilgrims.

One of the more popular practices to come out of the organisation of pilgrimages has been walking to Apparition Hill through the fields and vineyards with the guides while praying the rosary.

In 1997 it was a very special experience when walking through these fields coincided with the bells of the church of St James ringing out the Angelus. The sound of these bells is unique.

The spires of the church of St James could be seen from anywhere in the fields. They guided us and we could not get lost. Many of the vineyards are gone now and replaced by high rise apartments which block out the sight of the church spires. The Medjugorje of today is different but still special.

It is a place set apart from the rest of the world and because visitors are not glued to televisions etc, conversation is alive and inclusive. Medjugorje is a wind-down from the world. Before smartphones it was hard to know what was happening outside Medjugorje and most didn't want to know.

It is busy with lots to do, see and experience, hills and mountains to climb (if you can), but despite all the activity, even the get-togethers in restaurants after the evening prayer programme, sharing stories and laughter, the one enduring and abiding word I would choose to describe this little valley between the hills is … PEACE.

Chapter Three

THE VISIONARIES - THEN AND NOW

The story of that first day, 24th June 1981, and the six visionaries has been told and written about so many times I do not feel the need to re-write it. However, I do feel the need to remember that the six visionaries of that first day were not all the same six visionaries of the second day. On the 24th of June four girls, Ivanka, Mirjana, Vicka and Milka, and two Ivans (one 16 one older) saw Our Lady. She did not speak. They were scared and ran away.

On the 25th of June Ivanka, Mirjana, Vicka and 16 year old Ivan returned to the same spot. The older Ivan did not, nor did Milka as she had chores. Her sister Marija went instead. She saw Our Lady that day as did little ten year old Jakov Colo. There were many people present to witness the events and it was the day she first spoke – the 25th of June is now recognised as Anniversary day.

So we have the visionaries of today, three of whom still see Our Lady on a daily basis, Ivan, Vicka and Marija, and three of whom will see Her on a yearly basis for the rest of their lives: Mirjana on the 18th of March, Ivanka on the 25th of June, Jakov on Christmas day. Marija is the one chosen to give a message to the world on the 25th of every month.

On that second day, the 25th of June 1981, why did Our Lady not choose to go with the four Visionaries from the first day who had returned? Why choose two more? Don't forget when the Blessed Mother came to Medjugorje she came not only as the Queen of Peace but also as a teacher.

She came to teach the six children, through them the village and through the village the world. Her plan was to endeavour to lead all mankind to her Son and it seems, looking back after so many years, that in order to carry out this plan she really needed all six. She would eventually give them six different missions to pray for.

Also on that second day all those years ago, no one could have foreseen the level of free will commitment she was asking of the six young people, not even themselves. Having only recently learned of Lourdes and Fatima and how long those apparitions lasted, the children probably thought Medjugorje would be the same. They asked her constantly in those early days would she return, until one day she asked them if they were tired of her, so they never asked again. They just accepted. They would suffer a lot in many ways, at the hands of the communist authorities who tried so hard to stop what was happening. They brought the children in almost daily for questioning. Sometimes they were gone from early morning until late at night, causing great worry for their families.

They were questioned by their own priests and their parish priest Fr Jozo Zovko who really, at the beginning, did not know what to believe until, in prayer, he was guided.

Mirjana, who lived in Sarajevo and who had been spending time with her grandmother in Medjugorje, was sent back to Sarajevo, away from the other five. Things were not easy for her or her parents in Sarajevo. Mirjana was expelled from school, questioned alone every day and at fifteen years old was declared an enemy of the state. Despite all they were put through, not one of the six could be made to deny what they were seeing.

At that time, being young teenagers approaching adulthood, they probably had plans for their futures, what they would do or be. Then this amazing event happens, and they are asked to make this huge commitment (without knowing for how long) and all six, even ten year old Jakov, said YES. They and all of us looking back after almost 40 years could never have known that the days, weeks, and months of those early years would not end quickly but for the visionaries would last a lifetime.

All of them married and raised families, at the same time never failing to carry out what was required of them by Our Lady, whatever she needed to help fulfil her plan. They never falter and how hard that must have been and continue to be while the whole world watches and some just wait for them to make a mistake. Could any of us live their lives? I doubt I could.

Chapter Four

FR JOZO ZOVKO - PARISH PRIEST

O n that eventful day in Medjugorje in 1981 Fr Jozo was not in the parish and did not return for some days. A thunderstorm had brought down the telephone lines so with no communication he had no idea what was happening in the village. Arriving back in Medjugorje and hearing of the events he didn't know what to think and after talking to the six young people he was no wiser.

In those first days the children were constantly being taken in by the authorities for questioning.

One particular day, Fr Jozo was in the church alone praying for guidance. It troubled him that the people seemed more concerned with going to the hill rather than the church. At that same time the soldiers had come again to take away the children. The people had warned the children, who began to run down the hill toward the church where Fr Jozo was praying. Fr Jozo, in the church, heard a very clear voice saying, 'go now and protect the children' and he did not hesitate. He opened the door of the church as the children came running around the corner crying for his help. He took them into the church for safety and opened the door again as the soldiers rounded the corner asking if he had seen the children. He said yes but they ran straight on.

That day all doubts were gone for Fr Jozo, and the apparitions took place inside the church, in safety, for many years. Fr Jozo protected the six visionaries from then on and in doing so became a target himself so it was not easy for him.

Spies were placed in his congregation to listen to him speak and report what they heard.

On the 15th of August 1981, The Feast of the Assumption, he gave a homily which did not please the communist authorities. As a result two days later, on the 17th of August, as he was preparing for morning mass he was arrested and taken away from Medjugorje.

In October 1981 he was sentenced to three and a half years in prison. The children and the village were devastated by what was happening to this holy man. However, Our Lady told the children Fr Jozo would be okay and she kept them informed of how he was doing in prison.

While in prison two extraordinary things happened; his cell door would never lock and even though all lights in the prison went off at a certain time Fr Jozo's cell was never without a light.

Our Lady did look after him, and in February 1983, Fr Jozo was released - over a year short of his full sentence. However, he was not permitted to return to Medjugorje itself while communism was in power. He was sent to Tihaljina (not far from Medjugorje) and became parish priest there. He did not return to Medjugorje until after the fall of communism in 1989, after which he could come and go at will and would always be there for Anniversary, Feast Days etc.

For a number of years, he was based in Siroki Brijeg (about forty minutes from Medjugorje) and it was to there that pilgrims would travel to listen to him tell the extraordinary story of his experiences. He remained in Siroki Brijeg until mid/late 2000's when he was sent to Zagreb where he has more or less retired.

He was born on the 19th March 1941 (The Feast of St. Joseph), one of ten children. He is almost 80 now and deserving of a peaceful retirement for he has served the Lord and his Blessed Mother well.

Chapter Five

FR SLAVKO BARBARIC

Fr Slavko Barbaric was born 1946 in Dragacina. After finishing primary school he went to secondary school in Dubrovnik. In Humac in 1965 he entered the Franciscan order and was ordained in 1971. He carried on studying and acquired an MA in Theology in 1978.

For the following five years he was engaged in pastoral work in Bosnia-Herzegovina after which he began studying again in Freiburg. It was in Freiburg in 1982 where he became a doctor of religious teaching and also became a psychotherapist. He carried on his priestly duties while studying. He worked as a student chaplain in Mostar through 1982-84 and was often persecuted by the communists for his work with young people. Even though the authorities may have tried, they could not stop Fr Slavko serving the pilgrims in Medjugorje. He served them well before and after he was officially transferred there in 1983.

He became friend and protector to the six vision-aries. He travelled (sometimes with Vicka) to many countries spreading Our Lady's messages. He remained in Medjugorje through the war years. He gave his time unsparingly to the pilgrims and touched so many with his spiritually uplifting talks which were never judgemental but gave hope and changed lives. He always drew large crowds. He did not have a lot of time for small talk, but for a person in trouble there was always the time needed.

Every moment of Fr Slavko's day was dedicated to answering Our Lady's call and helping her achieve what she needed most, the return of mankind to her Son. Fr Slavko was single-minded in knowing what his mission was. He spoke many languages. He founded Mother's Village as a home for children left orphaned as a result of the 1991-5 war. He eventually would provide care for the old and, along with a wonderful Irish lady, founded the Kay House, a refuge and safe place for victims of domestic abuse. There were many other organisations he instituted.

When Mother Elvira founded Cenacolo (the home for drug addicts) in Medjugorje, Fr Slavko became her friend and helper. He gave so much love and help to the boys, saying masses in Cenacolo and just being there to listen to them and help them to recover. There was also Domus Pacis where more severely affected addicts were cared for. Fr Slavko always tried to find work they were capable of doing. No one was left out or forgotten.

He led the late Adoration in the church in a most unusual and holy way. In those days, the late 90s, the boys from Cenacolo led the music. He was responsible for instituting the youth festival which started with a few hundred people and now can bring 60-70,000. It is not possible to list all those people this priest cared for. His love for and his commitment to Mary and Her Son is unquestionable. I often wonder about Fr Slavko and sleep. When did he sleep? Let's recap on what we know of his daily routine.

He woke at 4.00 or 5.00am, a very early start. We know he climbed Cross Mountain and Apparition hill on alternate days collecting the rubbish left by pilgrims. As he was coming down, he would meet the first pilgrims going up. He would greet them and, according to the guides, he would often say, referring to his black bag, 'Look after the nature, for nature belongs to God'.

At 7.30am there was an early morning mass in St James's Church and with the job on the mountains done, Fr Slavko was there.

There is no exact timeline for the rest of his day but what is known of his daily routine is as follows: two/three mornings a week, after 7.30am mass he would go to Cenacolo where he would celebrate mass with the boys and spend time with them. Then on to Domus Pacis to check with the boys there and work out their day.

Every day he visited Mother Village where the children loved to see him, sometimes maybe have lunch with them if time permitted; however, there was never enough time and still lots to do.

Generally, a few days a week there were talks with the pilgrims. He hosted a radio program teaching the bible to children through the media.

On Sundays he climbed Apparition Hill with locals and pilgrims.

On Fridays he climbed Cross Mountain with locals and pilgrims. During the evening prayer program, which in summertime starts at 6.00pm, he was in his confession box until mass started at 7.00pm. In those days late Adoration was held on Wednesdays and Saturdays from 10.00-11.00pm. In the late 90s Fr Landeka, parish priest of Medjugorje at that time, once said of Fr Slavko, 'no minute of his day was wasted and sometimes after the late Adoration he would have a coffee with the other priests before retiring around midnight.'

So, I ask – retire to what? Sleep? If so, how much sleep? His day would start in a few hours, climbing the hill and mountain again. I doubt there was much sleep for we must remember his writing, all those wonderful books, translated into twenty different languages. He certainly did not write them during the day. So when?

He died on the 24th of November 2000 and the last day of his life started as all other days with his usual chores. He said mass for a small group of German pilgrims. As it was November there were very few pilgrims in the village, so things were quiet. He did as he always did on Fridays, lead parish and pilgrims to say the Stations on Cross Mountain. It was cold and raining but by the time they reached the top the rain had stopped and the sun was out. Fr Slavko prayed at the top with the people for a short while then stood and walked around the cross one last time, starting down the mountain. Reaching the 14th Station, he chose his spot, lay down and very gently surrendered his soul to God.

What a welcome he must have received in Heaven - and oh what sorrow and loss in Medjugorje on hearing the news. It was one of those occasions I remember exactly where I was when I heard and what I felt. Shock, devastation, disbelief. Three weeks previously I had been in Medjugorje in his presence having no idea it would be the last time. A sad day for us but not for him.

The following day, the 25th of November, the wonderful message came through Marija that Fr Slavko was in Heaven interceding for us.

Despite it being November and travel extremely difficult, 20,000 people attended his funeral on Sunday the 26th of November.

Fr Slavko was called home before fulfilling all his dreams and plans for Medjugorje but his passing made no difference as these dreams and plans continue to be carried out by those left behind.

He lies now in peace in the graveyard at the end of the walkway behind the church, in the triangle of the church, Apparition Hill and Cross Mountain where he would want to be. His resting place is always busy but peaceful - a beautiful place to rest a while in prayer and reflection.

I have been privileged so many times in my life but one of the greatest privileges has been knowing, listening to and learning so much from Fr Slavko.

May he continue to intercede for us and rest in peace.

Chapter Six

MY FIRST GROUP - MAY 1998

I

n May 1998, with the help of Marian Pilgrimages I brought my first group to Medjugorje.

I was 62 years of age and although I had organised various events over the years, I had never undertaken anything on the scale of a full pilgrimage before. I was nervous and discussing the matter with Tom Field in Marian Pilgrimages, he had asked whether I would bring a parish pilgrimage or an 'open to all' pilgrimage? Deciding on the latter I put my name in the Medjugorje magazine, *The Medjugorje Herald*, put my trust in the Blessed Mother, waited for the phone to ring – and it did.

In that first group I accompanied twenty eight people, six of whom I already knew. I had never met any of the others, not even the priest who had been recommended by a friend, as none of the priests I knew could travel at that time. My first group of pilgrims came from all over Ireland. A pattern would be set for the following twenty three years until the present.

We met the Marian Pilgrimage guides at Split airport. The first time the group was all together was on the bus from the airport to Medjugorje.

Philip Ryan, who at that time worked for Marian Pilgrimages in Medjugorje, accompanied us on that first bus journey. We said the rosary and Philip told the story of how Medjugorje started, the visionaries, and his own story. He gave us an appetite for more and arriving in Medjugorje some three to four hours later, although very tired, we were all in good spirits, me still nervous.

That first time we stayed in "Cilic" house which is quite close to the church of St James. As we settled in our rooms and prepared for our first meal together as a group (dinner that first evening), I wondered how I would cope with meeting twenty two people I had never met before. I could go to the dining room in the company of the six people I already knew or I could go alone and hope for the best. I went alone. I went to the dining room early and sat alone waiting for whoever came and sat beside me. Gradually the others came, and I found myself surrounded by strangers. I introduced myself as their group leader and by the end of that first week twenty two new friendships were made. I realised that if I were to be a group leader I would have to be prepared not to surround myself with my own friends (which would have been so easy) but to just be there for everybody, to listen to everybody, for most have stories to tell and problems to share. Many go on pilgrimage seeking comfort and help with their problems. Because of this, "Mixing" would become a big thing in my groups. Changing tables constantly and encouraging others to do the same, welcoming first timers and making them part of the group would always be important. That was a decision I made at that very first dinner.

At that time there was no Yellow Hall so our opening meeting took place at what is now known as 'The Outside Altar' and even though it was 'The Outside Altar' then it was also called 'The Dome'. It was there we were greeted on that first morning (the whole Marian Pilgrimage group) by Philip Ryan and the guides, Jozo and Claudia. Philip told more of the story of Medjugorje, made us aware of what to expect from the week's programme, the rules of the parish, English Mass times, evening prayer programme, etc.

It was a very busy week with so many highlights, the evening prayer programme, late night Adoration, the talks, meetings with four of the visionaries that week, walking through the fields praying the rosary, climbing Apparition Hill and Cross Mountain with the local dogs following the pilgrims as they climbed;

the whole atmosphere was amazing. The extraordinary thing about these same dogs was that during the evening programme and late Adoration (when it was held on the outside altar) as the gentle music drifted into the night air, they came to the steps of the altar and there rested quietly through the whole programme. It was really something to see.

Even the dogs sensed something special about this place.

I came home from that first experience as group leader knowing it was what I wanted to do for the rest of my life, however long or short that life would be or for however long Our Lady wanted me to do it. All I needed was the strength and that had to come from the Lady who started it all, and from her Son.

Chapter Seven

MY SECOND AND THIRD
GROUPS 1998

I n October 1998 I travelled again to Medjugorje intending to spend three weeks there, staying in Tomato House, bringing two groups back to back. The third week would be the last week of the Marian Pilgrimage season.

They had arranged a group leaders' week. During this week Tom Glynn and Tom Field, senior management of Marian Pilgrimages, would join the leaders in Medjugorje and come together in the local hotel one evening with the owners of the houses. It was their way of saying 'thanks' to the group leaders. They also extended thanks to our hosts in the houses and the team in Medjugorje. As I was a novice leader, I looked forward to spending time with veteran group leaders and learning more.

During that first week, on the second day, we climbed Apparition Hill. After praying a while seated on a rock I stood up to descend the hill. I tripped and as I fell my left wrist hit a rock and I felt it snap. Philip Ryan very carefully got me down the hill and along with Mojca, the guide, took me to Mostar hospital. They x-rayed the wrist, told me it was fractured, set it in plaster, gave me the x-rays and in thirty minutes we were on our way back to Medjugorje. I had no pain or discomfort for the rest of the week, and all went well with the group.

The day before my first group was due to return home and my second group were arriving, we were up at the base of Apparition Hill in Bijakovici early in the morning to hear Vicka (the eldest of the Visionaries) speak when Philip Ryan approached me and told me he felt I should go home with my group the following day and get a second opinion on my wrist.

Because I felt fine, I was annoyed and told him, 'no way'. I wanted to be in Medjugorje for my second group. It was while Vicka was praying for a long time in that extraordinary way she does, that I became really calm and decided to take Philip's advice. After the meeting with Vicka I told Philip who said he would make sure my group arriving would be okay and he would look after them. I told him I still intended to return for the group leaders' week.

In Dublin the wrist was reset, and I did return to Medjugorje as promised.

That leaders' week in Medjugorje in October 1998 was really special. Tom Glynn looked after us so well and I made many new friends among the leaders. Chief among these new friends were Paul Wallace (around my own age) and Michael Buffini (about 20 years younger), both veteran group leaders. They were staying in the same house as me and they became my 'meat cutters' doing so many things for me that I couldn't do because of my wrist. It was the beginning of a friendship which would last through the years. I was privileged they took me under their wing. That week was very special, spiritual but also filled with so much laughter and joy.

Paul would eventually become Chairperson of the National Medjugorje Council of Ireland and his story is a story to be told (see chapter Eight). Michael continued to bring groups for a number of years, but now travels yearly with only his wife and brother. Friendships made in this special place, I find, are friendships which last and grow stronger with time.

Chapter Eight

PAUL WALLACE- HIS STORY

Referring back to 1998, and my first meeting with Paul Wallace and Michael Buffini who were such a source of help to me. Lasting friendships were made with these two experienced group leaders and I realised if ever a story needed telling, it is Paul Wallace's story. With the blessing of his wife, Clodagh, and his daughter Sara, I will endeavour to do so.

In 1986 Paul and his wife Clodagh were involved with a cycling club where they lived in Glasthule, Co. Dublin. The cycling club was made up of young teenagers and the group travelled, fully eequipped with everything needed and accompanied by their own cook and navigator. They had already been to Rome, Lourdes and Garabandal. In 1986 they chose Medjugorje for their destination. On that occasion they travelled with twenty/thirty young cyclists. Reaching Humac in the days before 'sat nav' they were not sure of their way to Medjugorje. Stopping to ask directions from an old lady walking the road, she insisted on getting into the car with them to direct them herself.

She brought them right to the church of St. James where she got out of the car leaving large bunches of grapes in the car for them.

In Medjugorje they met Fr Slavko who greeted them warmly. This priest who always had time for young people allowed them to pitch their tents right behind the church where the outside altar is now.

While there, they met the visionaries and they stayed two nights. Those two nights in Medjugorje impressed Clodagh and left her wanting to go back. Paul, not so much. Paul, who had been away from the church and confession for a long time, was not thinking this way at all.

Because of Clodagh's need to go back, Paul accompanied her on pilgrimage two years later in 1988, although still not wanting to be there.

One morning, in the church during the English mass, Paul felt himself being physically pulled out of the church and a great need to go to confession. Leaving the church, he found a priest standing outside went up to him and said, 'I think Our Lady wants you to hear my confession'. With no hesitation, the priest asked Paul to walk with him and during that very special walk Paul made his first confession in years and returned after many years to his faith and his church. He would work so hard for that faith for the rest of his life.

Clodagh, on that pilgrimage in 1988, had an experience of her own to relate.

One evening on Apparition Hill while waiting with the crowd for Ivan's apparition she saw the crucifix, to the left of where Our Lady's statue is now, change shape and a wonderful golden light appear. Within the light she saw a Celtic motif. This motif was exactly the same motif which is in front of the altar in her local church in Glasthule in Ireland. She did not question this strange happening but felt that she personally was being asked or told that she was to do something at home in Ireland in her own parish. Shortly after returning home Clodagh decided to form a choir of young teenagers. This proved a very successful venture and in time she and Paul would get all of these young people to Medjugorje for the youth festival. Most of them are still active in the church today.

Paul was also instrumental in getting all of his children to Medjugorje and five of his grandchildren - and I know that to do this was one of his greatest wishes when I met him in 1998.

Clodagh relates an experience they both had that same year 1988. Walking back through the fields one evening in the dark after an apparition they met a very small man who appeared to be Indian. Pointing to Cross Mountain he said to them in an American accent, 'Have you seen the Phenomenon?'

Looking in the direction of where he was pointing, they counted fifteen bright blue lights with a white light pulsating in the centre of each light. The lights were zig-zagging from the base of the mountain to the top, and at the top two white lights were very close together. The man said, 'Those are my angels guarding the stations'. When they turned to look at the man again, he had gone, just vanished. Being a bit sceptical they did not know what to make of this and questioned, 'Why were there fifteen lights when there are only fourteen stations and why were they zig-zagging as they were?'. When they actually climbed cross mountain themselves for the first time a few days later, they realised three important things. The path through the stations does zig-zag all the way to the top. There are fifteen stations, they start with the Agony in the Garden, and finish at the top; the resurrection and the cross are close to each other and these were the two white lights. They also realised that, at that time in 1988, on Cross Mountain there was no electricity.

They then believed the man they spoke to when referring to, 'my angels' was the Lord himself. This experience may be hard for some to believe but if you really know Medjugorje, nothing is hard to believe.

He and Clodagh brought their first group to Medjugorje in 1989 and have brought groups every year up to and including 2019.

Paul would eventually become Chairperson of the National Medjugorje Council of Ireland and would, until the year 2020, organise the travel and accommodation arrangements for those going to Medjugorje for the international leaders week every year. I was privileged to attend with him and other group leaders on a number of occasions until age and health problems made it difficult for me to travel in harsh weather.

Shortly after returning from the early 2020 trip, Paul had to have emergency heart surgery. Unfortunately, he did not recover. He was called from this world on the 7th of April, Easter week, and to me no greater time for him to be called. He was a Cantor in his church and for years he sang through all the Easter ceremonies.

2020 was the year we first had COVID-19, with churches closed, no celebrating the Resurrection season, no joy, no singing for Paul; I do believe there was joy somewhere for Paul.

I believe Paul sang the Easter season with the choirs in Heaven in the presence of the Resurrected One himself and his Blessed Mother, for whom he worked so hard for so many years. May he Rest In Peace and may every joy and blessing be on his wife Clodagh and his family. May Sara, his daughter, who intends to carry on his work in Medjugorje, be blessed in this work.

Chapter Nine

WILLIE'S STORY

When I had the experience on Apparition Hill in 1997 which prompted me to bring groups to Medjugorje, I never expected anything personal to happen again. Telling this story necessitates telling some more of my personal story.

When I married Bill in 1962, he was a widower with four children. He had married very young, had been left a widower young, and had moved back in with his parents who actually raised his children. He came from a very large family with a few older sisters so there was, thank God, no shortage of help in the situation. In 1962, the year we were married, the children's ages ranged from fourteen to eighteen, the eldest boy and eldest girl already in relationships and there was no way they were going to leave their grandparents to live with us.

Bill and I eventually had two sons of our own.

I had become very close to Bill's eldest son Willie, who in 1998 (a year after his dad died) was a very heavy drinker. He had turned his back on the church and God in 1979 when his older sister, with whom he was very close, died on the birth of her fifth child. She was thirty-five, and her loss was too much for him.

A year after Bill died I moved house and, as Willie worked in construction (as did Bill and my own younger son), he gave me a lot of help renovating and decorating the house I bought in East Wall. Having just lost Bill a year earlier we talked a lot and one day during one of these chats, out of the blue Willie said, 'Carmel the next time you are going to Medjugorje I want to go with you'. Shock does not even cover what I felt at this statement, and I asked him if he had been drinking to which he responded, 'Well actually I was sitting on the high stool in the pub the other night with a pint in front of me when I suddenly got the urge to go to Medjugorje.'

So he and his wife Olive joined me in my second group in October 1998 (the week I broke my wrist) and I believe he was having second thoughts - for in the departure lounge at Dublin airport, he told me he would not be saying rosaries, going to mass or into the church, how after so much time, he could not see himself change. And I just said, 'No worries, I certainly will not be putting pressure on you or telling you what to do, I am only the group leader and it is certainly not because of anything I did that you are coming to Medjugorje - so you just do your own thing'.

The first full day in Medjugorje Willie went missing. He did nothing with the group. When he did not turn up in time for dinner his wife was convinced he was in a pub. Halfway through dinner Willie arrived, sober, sweaty, a big smile on his face and tells us he climbed Cross Mountain after breakfast and stayed there all day. He seemed very much at peace and content. The second day he was missing again and when he arrived just as dinner was starting I asked if he had been up Cross Mountain and he replied, 'Yes it's so peaceful up there. The best thing was, I came back through the church grounds and there was a priest hearing confessions in English so I went to confession to him'. I asked how he felt and he replied, 'I feel really great for I got twenty years of baggage off my shoulders'. That was the beginning of a whole new life for him - and I had done nothing!

That second evening after his confession experience, he joined me for the evening prayer programme. As the church was packed and it was a beautiful evening we decided to sit outside on a little wall by the main door of the church. The programme was being relayed outside. After about ten minutes Willie whispered to me, 'Do you mind if I go into the church?'. The same guy who told me no way was he going into a church was now going into a church. I told him, 'No problem - off you go' and watched him enter the church for the first time in twenty years. His wife who joined me a while later could not believe what she was seeing as the programme ended and her husband walked out of the church.

The rest of the week he stayed with the programme, drastically cut down on his drinking, never missed mass, and on returning home never missed regular confession. He returned to Medjugorje many times after that and spent a lot of time helping Sr. Muriel in her care of the old, doing odd jobs and anything that needed doing.

He would eventually lead the rosary in his own parish church every morning after mass before being stricken a few years ago with an aggressive form of dementia. He is now in a home and knows no one, recognises none of his family, and it is not easy for them.

Talking to his son Stuart recently about telling his dad's Medjugorje story he said how much he would love just ten minutes in his dad's company, having normal conversation.

Olive too, unfortunately also suffering from Dementia, is in a different home to Willie. She does not even remember she has a husband.

The Lord's plan is not always easy to accept but in faith we must trust in Him to help us when times of trial come. What comes to my mind in relating this story is that in 1998 in Medjugorje Willie returned to the God and the Church he had abandoned twenty years previously. After his return to his faith he served this same God and Church faithfully for twenty years before dementia struck him. I can only ask the Lord at this point to grant him and his wife Olive peace of mind in their illnesses and to ease the pain of their five children and the grandchildren they no longer know.

Chapter Ten

MEDJUGORJE AND THE KOSOVO WAR 1999

In 1999 the war in Kosovo was raging and the proximity of Kosovo to Bosnia-Herzegovina and Medjugorje caused a lot of people to decide to either not book for Medjugorje or cancel bookings already made.

I travelled in June 1999 myself, with only eight others and we stayed again in Tomato House. It was hard to believe how quiet the village was. There were one hundred and sixty five Irish people in Medjugorje that week. There were no English, German, Italian, French or American pilgrims, although their planes were flying over Medjugorje to bomb Kosovo.

There was no need for the seats to be out at the back of the church, which seems strange in June. We had Medjugorje to ourselves and while it was certainly unusual, it was a wonderful experience.

Also staying in Tomato House that week were several individuals. It was my privilege to meet, for the first time, Ken Parkes (son of David who would eventually work for Marian Pilgrimages). Ken was there with his mother Anne, They were there with Youlande Kelly and some other relatives and friends. Youlande Kelly was the wife of Des Kelly the carpet man. Des had several carpet and furniture stores all over Dublin and he and Youlande, both deceased now RIP, were great workers for Medjugorje and Des also for the homeless in Dublin. Des had also worked very hard with Cenecalo in Ireland and Medjugorje.

That week was extremely hot with very little air, and Ken who suffered from Cystic Fibrosis struggled to breathe. Despite how hard it was for him he was always in good form and never complained. He was watched over very carefully by his mother Anne, a very Special Lady.

Ken eventually had a double lung transplant in November 2002 which, thank God, gave him a number of years of good health before in 2016 things changed again.

Youlande Kelly gave us many a laugh that week with her great sense of fun. It is strange at times the way the Lord works for I could not know then there would be times in the future when Ken Parkes would play a role in my life, nor could I know I would have many encounters with Youlande and Des Kelly in Medjugorje. They had an apartment and spent quite a bit of time there.

Youlande passed away in October 2013, RIP. My last encounter with Des himself was in July 2016. We were both in Medjugorje the same week. I didn't see anything of Des during the week as he did very much his own thing, I know he did climb that week.

Temperatures were in the forties and the day we were returning home at Dubrovnik airport I was really struggling in the heat to pull my case up the ramp to departures. I was actually silently praying to the Lord to help me get to the top, when suddenly the case was taken out of my hand by Des Kelly. I was so thankful to see him and I told him the Lord had sent him. He laughed and commented on both of us getting too old. I joked about being older than him and he told me how he hoped to spend more time in Medjugorje in the future as he had retired from the company completely. That was his plan, but the Lord had a different plan for less than one week later, Des had been called to join Youlande. Their work was done.

I encountered Ken Parkes again, not so many times but each time very special, and on every occasion it seemed as though he had been sent to help when I needed help the most. He will know the conversations we shared meant so much to me and he holds a very special place in my heart. Getting to know Anne and Ken in 1999, I realised I was meeting those closest to the man whose music had brought such comfort to my husband in his last days. The man who would in 2001 be working for Martian Pilgrimages in Medjugorje; David Parkes.

Chapter Eleven

MILLENNIUM IN MEDJUGORJE

As the millennium approached all the talk was about celebration, the best way to celebrate the ending of the 1900s and the beginning of the 2000s. There was talk of the breakdown of technology and planes falling out of the sky. Of course, thank God, none of this happened. The transition from one year to the next, one millennium to the next, went smoothly amid much partying and joy.

I am not really a party person but did want to do something special to mark the occasion. I knew where I wanted to be. I wanted to be in Medjugorje to see in the year 2000. I expressed my wish to Tom Fields in Marian Pilgrimages as I also had a few friends wanting to go to Medjugorje. However, when Tom put the idea out there, there was not a great response. He did discover there was a small group of pilgrims in England with the same idea, so he arranged for the six of us Irish to join eight from England and fly from London, fourteen in all.

Travelling to Medjugorje was a pilgrimage in itself! We flew to London to meet the group, then flew to Zagreb, Zagreb to Split, then the bus journey to Medjugorje. We were totally exhausted on arrival at our destination which was one of the English houses in Medjugorje.

Medjugorje at the new year was completely different to the Medjugorje we were used to in the summertime. It was bitterly cold, a cold which really got into your bones.

Every bed in Medjugorje was full. There were heaters in every room but because of the crowds in the village our host asked us to use them sparingly or not at all for fear of the system breaking down. Obviously very few listened, as on the second day that is exactly what happened. No electricity at all in the village, even the church. They did have generators so for the rest of the week we listened to the 'chug, chug' of these generators as the village struggled. In our house the generator provided lights to only one half of the house on alternate nights and no heat at all. We did not get warm during that week even in bed as the cold was so intense. It really was a true pilgrimage.

Meanwhile, Masses, evening prayer programme, Adoration, all the usual events associated with Medjugorje carried on as usual and were relayed into the yellow hall which was full to capacity. Despite the cold and the discomfort of that week laughter and joy were not lacking.

On New Year's Eve night itself, Mass started in the church at 11pm. Fr Slavko was the main celebrant (he could not know it would be his last new year). Some of us, for lack of seats, stood by the wall in the church for a long time. Mass was not over until 12.30am.

What was most beautiful was hearing at midnight the bells of the Consecration ring at exactly the same time the bells in the steeple rang in the year 2000. The boys from Cenacolo provided the music at Mass and afterwards set up on the steps of the church and entertained us for quite a while. Despite the cold, the atmosphere was amazing, the experience unforgettable and I knew there was nowhere else I would rather be.

Getting to know and chat with that group that week I became very friendly with one of the English ladies named Angela who was expressing regrets about making the trip and was really unhappy. Finally, one day, managing to get into a real conversation with her, she told me that because of a bad relationship with her own mother, she could never relate to or have any time for the Blessed Mother. She could not relate to Our Lady in any way. Talking to her did no good.

She did not want to be there. This was to change, for a few days before we were due to leave, we were invited to hear Fr Slavko speak. Angela, being very impressed with this priest and what he had to say, whispered to me, 'I would like to go to confession to him.' Realising how important this was, as she hadn't been to confession for years, after the talk I introduced her to Fr Slavko and left them alone. He told her to come to his confession box in the church that evening before mass and he would hear her confession.

She did go and told me later she actually went on the attack as soon as she entered the box, saying to Fr Slavko, 'Before we start you need to know I have no time for our Lady.' Fr Slavko asked her in his very gentle way, 'Have you time for Jesus?' to which she replied, 'Yes, I have no problem with Jesus' and he responded, 'Well that's okay then because that's all Our Lady wants. She wants us to have time for her Son. She wants nothing for herself but for Him.' Hers was the last confession he heard that day and they came out of the box together. Outside he asked her what her occupation was. She told him she was a dental technician and Fr Slavko, being in charge of Mother's Village, asked if she would consider giving a few months of her time to checking the teeth of the children in the village. Taken off guard, she could see no way of managing to do this.

The last few days of that week saw Angela become a different person. She was content and at peace. On the plane returning to England she approached me and told me that, while in that year 2000 she couldn't help Fr Slavko, she would make sure in 2001 to arrange to give him the time he needed. Unfortunately, this was not to be as the Lord called Fr Slavko home on the 24th November 2000.

Chapter Twelve

MARY AND MORGAN'S STORY

Colette from Galway was a regular returnee to Medjugorje. She had a wish she prayed hard for, that her younger sister Mary would one day join her in Medjugorje. Her prayer was answered in May 2002 when Mary did join Colette on pilgrimage. Mary could not know that on this trip, a plan would be set in motion which would change the course of her life completely.

At that time the pilgrims were taken to Siroki Brijeg to see and hear Fr Jozo(parish priest of Medjugorje at the time of the apparition). He told, through the translator, Nancy Latta, of his experiences and of how he was made to suffer for his beliefs.

Fr Jozo was also known to have extraordinary gifts of discernment and healing when he prayed over people. After his talk it was the custom for the people to line the aisles for the prayers of healing. Because of the crowd all the visiting priests were asked to assist (which they did) but most people hoped to be in Fr Jozo's line. Many rested in the spirit and healings, both spiritual and physical, took place.

It was on this trip things would change for Mary. On the bus to Fr Jozo that day Mary was seated beside a lad she did not know. Starting a conversation he asked where she was from. When she replied, 'Galway' he asked, 'Where is that?' Thinking he was Irish she responded more or less, 'Come on you don't know where Galway is?' and he replied, 'Why would I, I'm from New York'. From there they got into an easy conversation all the way to the destination and he told her his name was Morgan.

During the healing service in Siroki Brijeg both Mary and Morgan were in Fr Jozo's line. Mary stood in line beside a lad from Kerry who stood between her and Morgan. When Fr Jozo reached them he put his right hand on Mary's head and his left on the head on the lad from Kerry, prayed a moment and then did a very unusual thing. Remember Fr Jozo did not know these people, had never met them before, but saying nothing, he moved the Kerry lad to the other side of Morgan and moved Morgan beside Mary, prayed over the two of them together and moved on. What did Fr Jozo discern when praying with these two young people? Time would tell. On the way back to Medjugorje on the bus Morgan and Mary continued to get to know each other.

On arrival in Medjugorje and about to go their separate ways, Morgan invited Mary to meet him for a coffee that evening. They met and the friendship developed. On parting to return to their respective countries, they exchanged phone numbers and addresses and agreed to keep in touch.

They did keep in touch over the following years and what started with a meeting on a bus in Medjugorje in 2002 culminated in a wedding in New York in 2005.

They are still an united and very happily married couple now living in Texas. Colette's prayers for Mary to join her in Medjugorje succeeded and Mary's life changed completely. Fr Jozo was obviously inspired to place Mary and Morgan side by side that afternoon in his church and in doing so enabled the Lord's plan in their lives to be fulfilled.

Mary returned to Medjugorje with Colette in 2006 in thanksgiving.

PICTURE 1. Marian Pilgrimages Group, September 2014.

PICTURE 2. Marian Pilgrimages Group, May 2009.

Picture 3. Marian Pilgrimages Group, May 2008.

PICTURE 4. Vicka and Carmel, 2002.

PICTURE 5. "A very, very quiet Medjugorje due to Kosovo", June, 1999.

PICTURE 6.
Arm in a sling, October 1998.

PICTURE 7.
Fr Slavko, October 2000, one month before his death.

PICTURE 8.

Mirjana, September 1999.
"On this occasion she spoke in English and we were so close and Sam was excited."

PICTURE 9.

Vicka, June 1999.

PICTURE 10.
David and Fr Donal, "So relaxed". Cenaclo 20/05/09.

PICTURE 11.
Vicka and Anne, June 1999.

PICTURE 12.

"Self 7th Station", May 1999.

PICTURE 13.
Fr Slavko, May 1998.

PICTURE 14.

Carmel with Joan Ashbrook - not dated.

PICTURE 14.

Cenaclo group (see Chapter 6).

PICTURE 16.

Rita Fitzgerald and
Paul Wallace, June
1999.

PICTURE 17.

Ozana, Marian
Pilgrimages Guide,
May 2004.

PICTURE 18.

Vladka, Marian Pilgrimages Guide, taking a group up the mountain.

PICTURE 19.

Danijela, Marian Pilgrimages Guide, enjoying the Group Leaders' party at the end of the season.

Paul Wallace and David Parkes. International Leaders Week,
February 2001.

Pilgrims enjoying breakfast in Tomato House, Medjugorje, 2000.

PICTURE 22.

Anne & Ken Parkes, June 1999

PICTURE 23.

Tom Glynn, Marian Pilgrimages founder & MD, getting involved in the
sing-song at the Group Leader's party in Medjugorje.

PICTURE 24.

'In reflection'
Carmel's Son, Willie Kelly on Cross mountain, May 1999.

Picture 25.
'Myself after a long climb'
Carmel on Cross mountain, May 1999.

Quotations in the picture captions taken
from the words of Carmel written on the
back of the original photographs.

Chapter Thirteen

FRANK'S STORY

In 2002 Frank, a Scotsman, was living and working in Ireland. His wife Madeleine still lived and worked in Scotland but spent every other weekend in Ireland with Frank. Their son Francis lived in Ireland also. Only a year before, in 2001, Frank and Madeleine had lost their younger son Kevin to cancer at thirty-one years of age. Naturally they were as devastated as all parents would be. However, they were people of faith. Someone in Scotland, a friend of Madeleine, had spoken to her about Medjugorje and Madeleine decided she really wanted to go there. She could find no information in her home place of Glasgow so she asked Frank what he could find out in Ireland. As the Lord would have it, my cousin Maura had been to Medjugorje with me in 1998, and Maura happened to work with Frank.

One day, mentioning Madeleine's wish to visit Medjugorje to Maura, she informed him she had a cousin who brought groups and, giving him my number, told him to ring me. He did. After talking at length on the phone that first time, he said he would ring me back after talking to Madeleine. A few days later he contacted me again and booked two places to travel in June 2002, one place for Madeleine and one other, no name yet. I asked was he not coming himself to Medjugorje to which he responded, 'Not with all those "Holy Marys"!' (this was a phrase I would hear often in respect to Medjugorje). 'No', he said, 'Madeleine can bring her sister or one of her friends'.

I often say, 'We make plans and God laughs' for certainly this was a time when Frank's plans were not in sync with the Lord's plans. Madeleine's sister did not want to go to Medjugorje, nor did any of her friend's and as Frank did not want her travelling alone, he went with her. He was the one being called to this very special place, not any of Madeleine's friends.

The first evening in Medjugorje I brought the first timers on a walk: first of course, the church; the Risen Lord; Fr Slavko's grave; Our Lady's statue; the original church. I answered many questions to the best of my ability. I wanted them to have just a tiny flavour of the place and of the week to come. By the end of the week, Frank was definitely a Medjugorje person. He has returned every year since, sometimes twice a year, and even though they have sold up in Ireland

and returned to Glasgow, he always ensures he is in Medjugorje when my group is there.

He climbs Apparition Hill and Cross Mountain every day. After going to confession, to Fr Svet (a local priest sadly no longer in Medjugorje) who is an extraordinary confessor, Frank became a great friend and helper to him in his mission of caring for the children in Mother's Village. This had become part of Fr Svet's duty after Fr Slavko's death.

Frank is another who has been a great help to me personally. He has over the years managed to bring his son Francis, daughter-in-law Niamh, and three of his grandchildren to Medjugorje. He remains a great worker for Our Blessed Lady and her Son.

Chapter Fourteen

OCTOBER 2002 - WHEN I BECAME A PROJECT

After Fr Slavko's death on Cross Mountain in November 2000, a memorial stone was carried up by the boys from Cenacolo and placed on the spot where he had died. I had climbed Cross Mountain only once,with help, in 1998.

I knew, because of age and health problems I would never climb it again and I was okay with that. However, while in Medjugorje in October 2002 with my last group of the season, I casually expressed a longing, while chatting with the group, to see the stone as I had such high regard for this very special priest. Having voiced this longing, I thought no more about it, but that was not to be the end of it.

To my complete surprise and amusement, two of the group - Colette, my stalwart returnee, and her friend Liz - approached me the following day and told me they were making me their "Project" for the week. These two ladies were a lot younger than me, very fit and veteran climbers. When I enquired what they meant by making me their "Project" they explained, 'It is our project this week to get you up Cross Mountain to see Fr Slavko's memorial stone.' I laughed, I thought it was the funniest thing I had ever heard, but they were not laughing. They were serious and determined.

When I tried to tell them how slow I would be, how long it could take, it made no difference. When they said they would go at my pace, I said I was willing to try. That same week Youlande and Des Kelly (RIP) were in Medjugorje and meeting them one day in Colombo's Restaurant. I told them of the "MAD" plan my two pilgrims had to get me up the mountain. Youlande especially, thought this was hilarious saying, 'Carmel you'll never do it!'

In October in Medjugorje the days are short and dinner is at 3.45pm. It was decided, by my two friends, that in order to achieve what they wanted to achieve, we would get the local 7.30am mass, have our breakfast in the house, then get a taxi to the foot of the mountain so I wouldn't be too tired. Two days later this is what we actually did. We were accompanied by two other members of the group, who, even though I told them it would be a very slow climb, were determined to join us.

I remember standing at the foot of Cross Mountain that cold crisp October morning around 9.00am and asking Our Lady for help in this undertaking and offering the climb to her, and of course, her Son. So with my four friends we began to climb.

We got to the third station without incident and while we were slow, I felt I was doing quite well. Then the skies opened, and the rain came down in torrents. We all had rain gear with us but being aware of the risks, I felt we should abandon the climb - either wait for the rain to stop or try to descend. Both Colette and Liz said, 'No way!' They were used to climbing and intended to go on. The other two pilgrims stated they were going on also. So, remembering to whom I had offered the plan and not wanting to try descending alone, I placed my trust in the Lord and carried on.

At the ninth station the rain did stop, and the sun came out. With the sun the ground began to dry out fairly quickly. It was a very slow and rewarding climb that day and we reached the Cross just as the bells in the church of St James, down in the valley, rang out the Angelus. We had been climbing for three hours and for me it was the greatest feeling in the world, reaching the top. We separated at the top, each of us finding a place to sit, to rest and pray a while, to savour and enjoy the peace and tranquillity which could be found in the proximity of the cross.

While there I reflected on the villagers who, back in 1933, to honour the nineteen hundredth anniversary of the death of Jesus, carried by hand, up to the top, everything needed to build this cross. Cement, steel, water and sand (not light materials) and they did it out of love. I was so blessed to be there that day.

I saw, and prayed by, Fr Slavko's memorial stone and then suggested we descend as dinner was at 3.45pm. My friends had other ideas, for at that point Liz said, 'Not before we feed you' and she produced sandwiches and a flask of tea. As we began our descent that day, I said a silent goodbye to the cross and that special place, for I knew I would never climb Cross Mountain again.

We arrived back at the house very tired, but I was, and still am, so grateful to the ladies who decided to make getting me up that mountain their "Project" that week.

That evening after the prayer programme, a few of us decided to go to Colombo's, not realising the word had spread that I had climbed Cross Mountain. As I entered Colombo's, from a table across the restaurant, came the voice of Youlande Kelly, really loud, 'Ah here comes "Mountain Carmel"!'.

From then on, I was always "Mountain Carmel" to Youlande even if she was calling me in the street, I would hear 'Mountain Carmel!'

God rest Youlande, and just as I remember my last encounter with her husband Des (RIP), I remember very clearly the last time I was together with Youlande in Medjugorje. It was the feast of Corpus Christi in 2011 and I met Youlande watching the procession leave the church grounds. Realising some of the First Communion children were in first communion dresses, while others were not, I remarked to Youlande how all of the children did not have dresses and she explained to me how really poor these people were. Not all in Medjugorje were wealthy. They could not afford these dresses. She then told me how she made a point of going around the shops in Dublin after first communions were finished in Ireland and bargaining for any dresses they did not want to keep. These dresses she brought to Medjugorje for the children who could not afford them. I was really amazed to hear this but when I tried to say how great I thought she was Youlande responded, laughing, 'Sure it's really nothing, carpets were good to us.' We walked in the procession together on a beautiful sunny summer evening, through the village past all the little altars outside many homes and businesses, and remembered times past when we experienced the same celebrations of this great feast in Ireland, and I felt sad. Arriving back in the church grounds the ceremonies continued and concluded there. Youlande and I, after a short stop in Colombo's restaurant, went our separate ways and that was the last time we spent real time together.

I was in Medjugorje in October 2013 when it was announced at the English mass that Youlande had passed away. It was a huge shock. Sisters and priests in the parish (especially Fr Svet, a very close friend of theirs) were shocked. Mass was celebrated for her in Mothers Village, for which she and Des were great workers. Because they are both gone I can speak about that work but when they were actually doing it, they did it as quietly as they could.

It is meeting people like the Kellys, Colette and Liz that makes being a group leader such a privilege and a joy. They are a blessing to me.

Chapter Fifteen

PETER'S STORY

By May 2004 I had brought many groups to Medjugorje and this work had really become my life. At times, the numbers were so big I filled Tomato House and also a second house. It did not take long to realise that for me, this was not feasible. Keeping in contact with the whole group whilst spread over two houses was impossible. I could only stay in one house so felt I was not doing right by the people in the second house. I decided I would keep the numbers down to what would fill one house.

It was in May 2004 that Peter and his daughter joined us. He was undergoing chemotherapy for very advanced cancer and had actually come to Medjugorje between two chemotherapy sessions and was quite ill. Every Thursday evening visiting priests are invited to be present during Ivan's apparition with Our Lady and sometimes very sick people are invited to attend also. On this occasion Peter was invited to be there.

Talking to him on his return from Ivan's he told me he felt his cancer was gone. Asking him what made him think that he responded, 'Just a feeling'. He was returning home the following day and he told me he intended to ask his consultant to redo all the tests necessary to determine what stage his cancer was at. He was also going to attend for his next chemotherapy session a few days after his return home. I told him I would call him when I was back in Ireland as I was staying in Medjugorje to greet another group arriving on the flight which was bringing him home.

I did ring him a few days after my return and he told me how resistant his consultant was at first about re-doing any tests as they felt they knew all they needed to know at that time. However, at Peter's insistence, he finally agreed to do the tests.

When the consultant called him into his office on receipt of the results of the tests, he told Peter his cancer was all gone, and he could not explain it. Peter queried him, 'What do you mean all gone?' and the consultant repeated, 'It's just all gone, there is no sign of any cancer!' And when Peter queried again what he meant by all gone the consultant getting frustrated, finally replied, 'Peter what part of "all gone" don't you understand.'

I was surprised at this response from Peter and I asked him, 'Why did you question when the expert confirmed what you told me you already felt?' His reply: 'Carmel, it's one thing to feel something has changed, and you hope that feeling is right - but it is another thing entirely when the cancer expert tells you that feeling is real, there is no cancer and that all is well.'

Peter continued to be well and cancer-free and returned to Medjugorje with his wife in thanksgiving in 2005.

Chapter Sixteen

ANNIVERSARY 2006

The year 2006 (25th Anniversary) I brought eleven groups to Medjugorje, the largest number of groups I would ever bring in a year. Bringing two groups back to back I was spending two weeks in Medjugorje, two weeks in Ireland, and back again. I realised this work really had become my life's work.

That week in June 2006 would be a week of extraordinary happenings. It was a troubled week but looking back also a very blessed week. There were thirty one of us in the group.

Amongst our number we had a young couple, Chris and Monica. Monica, twenty-six years of age and the mother of two young children, was dying of cancer. There was no hope for her. She was a really beautiful person. Her faith was so strong and meant everything to her. She was a joy to be around, never complaining and her young husband Chris could not do enough for her.

They were first timers. A few days into the pilgrimage it became obvious that among our number we had a person with serious behaviour problems who was causing a lot of disruption night and day in the group and it was apparent this behaviour would carry on through the week.

However, what I did come to realise as the week progressed, was how very much present the Blessed Mother and her Son were. At that time, Ken Parkes happened to be staying in Medjugorje with his dad David. As his dad was really busy every day, Ken was at a loose end and was spending most of his time with me and my group. Ken had undergone a double lung transplant in 2002 and in 2006 was a fit and healthy young man. As the situation in my group worsened (Monica getting sicker by the day and my troubled pilgrim getting no better) the load getting bigger for David and myself, I came to realise what a blessing the Lord had sent me in the person of Ken Parkes. Every morning after breakfast Ken arrived at Tomato House and stayed in my company all day every day to help in any way he could. In a very frazzled week, Ken's quiet nature helped to keep me calm and balanced.

Not long after the pilgrimage started, we realised Monica needed a wheelchair, and this was fine until we were all invited to be present with Ivan for an apparition at 10pm one evening at Blue Cross. Of course, this was something no one wanted to miss, certainly not Monica, but for her walking wasn't possible. We didn't need to worry as some of the men in the group carried Monica, wheelchair and all, up to the first level of Blue Cross, where she, her husband and myself remained, along with many others waiting for that special moment. As the apparition started Monica got out of the wheelchair and along with Chris and myself, stood on a little wall which enabled us to look over the wall in front of us in the direction of where Ivan was having his apparition. Anyone who has attended an apparition knows the total silence (no matter how large the crowd) surrounding these occasions and it was in this silence, at the top of his voice Chris cried out, 'She's going now'. I looked at Chris knowing he was having an experience and at the same time knowing Medjugorje was for Chris, not Monica. Returning to Tomato restaurant after the apparition, the three of us sat, two of us waiting very patiently for a very quiet Chris to speak. Eventually he did tell us how he had seen Our Lady leave and how he had watched her bless everyone as she left.

The following morning neither of them appeared for breakfast, so I knocked on the door to find Chris had already been in touch with the Mater hospital in Dublin as Monica had been in such pain throughout the night. The hospital had told him to get Monica home as quickly as possible and bring her straight to the hospital.

I called David who came immediately to the house and set the wheels in motion to get them both home that same day. He also called a local doctor who gave Monica an injection which enabled her to sleep. While she slept Chris and I sat outside talking and he questioned why he would see Our Lady and not Monica, 'After all, he said, she is the one with the faith, she goes to mass and says the rosary, I don't so why me?' I tried to explain to him that was the whole reason he saw Our Lady, he would be the one needing strength, not Monica; she already had it. Medjugorje was for him not her.

David drove them to Dubrovnik and that evening they flew back to Dublin and straight to the hospital. On my return I visited Monica in hospital where she had been told the cancer had spread. I also visited her at home and she spoke about how much she loved Medjugorje. She spoke about going back with Chris and the children but that was her dream and it would never happen. She passed away peacefully in early 2007 and I attended her funeral, which was a very large one. I believe Chris did eventually return to Medjugorje with the children.

Also in our group that week we had Teresa, who had been with me on a number of previous occasions. This time she came with her daughter Audrey and her grandson Aaron. After returning home, Teresa rang me regularly, as did many of the group, enquiring after Monica, and it was one of these occasions she relayed the following story to me of what happened to them that same week. She explained the reason she hadn't told the story at the time was because there was so much going on in the group.

On the same night of the apparition when Chris had seen Our Lady, Teresa, Audrey and Aaron had gone up really early to get a good position and were fairly close to Ivan when the apparition started. Then in the silence little Aaron began to call out, 'Holy Mary, Holy Mary'. It took Teresa (who was holding him on her lap) time to realise he could be seeing something. Teresa tells how while Aaron had his head turned into her chest he had one eye focused in the same direction Ivan's eyes were while saying, 'Holy Mary, Holy Mary' over and over.

She's sure that he saw Our Lady that night, that her nineteen month-old grandchild was seeing something she and her daughter could only sense. That same nineteen-month-old grandson has grown into a lovely young man now, one to be proud of.

Since my first time in Medjugorje and my one special experience on Apparition Hill, I had never personally had or needed any more personal unusual happenings. The group were being blessed and that was all I needed.

Also present with us this particular week was another regular pilgrim and friend - Colette. Walking back to the house from the church with her on a beautiful and very warm day, I told her how guilty I felt as I said, 'You know Colette I feel so bad, there is so much happening in the group but I don't seem able to pray this week.' Very gently she responded, 'Carmel, it's not your prayers she wants this week, it's your suffering.' At the time we were walking across the grassy area in front of the adoration chapel where there are no flowers when suddenly, in the warmth of the day, a beautiful gentle breeze passed on my left side, followed by the most incredible smell of roses I had ever experienced. I stopped dead and said to Colette, 'Did you get that?', 'Get what?' she asked. 'The smell of roses', I replied. 'No', she said 'I didn't but that's for you this week and not for me.' It was the only time in Medjugorje I would ever smell the roses.

It took some time after returning home for me and most of us, looking back, to realise how many blessings were actually bestowed on us that week. In the midst of what was, without a doubt, a very fraught week, I was never at any time without help. Ken and David were very much present, I had the understanding and patience of the rest of the group, and the gift of Monica in her suffering and how Chris cared for her. Most of all this was the realisation and certainty of the presence of Our Blessed Lady and her Son Jesus.

Chapter Seventeen

MAY'S STORY

May came to Medjugorje in 2009 for the first time in the company of family and friends who were already regular pilgrims. She came in a highly distressed state, seeking spiritual help where there seemed to be none. She was seeking help for herself, but especially for her daughter Judy, whose husband had recently taken his own life.

Neither Judy nor her mother were coping well with the situation, especially with the manner in which it had happened. Judy was home one day with her three children, ages six, four and one, when her husband rang her on his mobile, told her he was in the local park where he was about to hang himself, and that is what he did. She, being too far away, unable to leave her three young children, could do absolutely nothing to stop him. There was no time. It was a horrific situation for her, for the family and for her mother who wanted to help her daughter but did not seem able to.

However, that week May spent in Medjugorje would become a new beginning. That week away from home, in the presence of the Our Lady Queen of Peace and her Son, a week in which May cried a lot, spent hours in my company just talking, spent time also with David Parkes (when he could), would be a whole new beginning. She went home a different person and, thank God, her daughter eventually met someone new with whom she is very happy, and is now the mother of another beautiful baby boy.

May returned to Medjugorje in 2010 in thanksgiving. That could have been the end of May's story, but it wasn't.

In 2011 she returned with her daughter Michelle who was sixteen years old and has Down's Syndrome. Michelle, like all Down's Syndrome children, was and is a loving and cheerful girl but at that time suffered frequent epileptic seizures. These seizures were dangerous and exhausting for her and worrying and frightening for those who had to watch helplessly. Michelle loved Medjugorje and was taken to the hearts of all in the group who prayed hard for her that week. May was granted another great blessing: since returning from Medjugorje in 2011 Michelle has never experienced another epileptic seizure. She has been fit and well through all the years since. They returned, both mother and daughter, in 2012 in thanksgiving. May herself returns every year to the place that changed her life and the lives of her family when things looked so bleak.

Chapter Eighteen

MARK'S STORY

Rachel came to Medjugorje in 2006 with her friend Joan. Joan had been coming with me since 2000. She came with my May groups and had become a great help to me, because at that time the May groups were always large groups. Rachel felt she would like her husband Mark to experience Medjugorje, but not being sure whether Mark himself would want to experience Medjugorje, she had to figure out how to get him there.

And she did. Mark's fortieth birthday had already passed so Rachel decided she would bring him to Dubrovnik for the birthday which was already gone. Of course, Dubrovnik would really be Medjugorje. Arriving at Dublin Airport, Mark was excited about this trip to Dubrovnik when we were informed there would be a delay. That was okay until a few hours later, when we were informed of a further delay and nothing seemed definite. Those who lived in Dublin or close to the airport were told they could go home, and they would be called back as departure time approached. Some did avail of this opportunity. Some of those opting to stay in the departure area decided to pray the rosary. Mark at this time began to wonder why all these people going on holiday to Dubrovnik would be praying.

Questioning Rachel, he asked, 'Why are all these "Holy Marys" praying the rosary?' so Rachel had to admit that their destination was Medjugorje. Initially Mark was not pleased and felt he wanted to go home. Again, by the end of the week it was a case of another life changed and another story to be told.

When the group were invited during that week to be present at an apparition with Ivan, Mark and Rachel were quite close to Ivan. That night during the experience, Mark tells how he could not believe the silence when the apparition started. It seemed unreal. As time went on during the apparition, he felt something like a gentle breeze or touch across the back of his neck. Asking Rachel beside him, she described feeling exactly the same thing. Ivan explained when the apparition finished, that Our Lady, as she always did, blessed everyone on leaving - but that night a bit differently. It seemed as if She blessed everyone individually. Mark believes he felt her touch that night.

Mark has, since then, returned almost every year to Medjugorje with my September group and is a great source of help and a friend to me. He is also a gifted singer and guitarist and has become our resident entertainer. He is another who is always there if someone needs to be pushed in a wheelchair or needs help in any way.

In 2010 Mark and Rachel returned to Medjugorje and with Mark's brother Damien and Damien's partner Sandra, who had been together for a number of years. Damien wanted to propose to Sandra, so without telling her, he bought a ring and decided he would propose in Medjugorje. They were both first-timers. Being told of the opening meeting in the Yellow Hall the morning after the arrival, Damien felt that was where he wanted to propose. Knowing that the Marian Pilgrimage group was very large that week, and the Yellow Hall would be nearly full, I tried to dissuade him but he was determined, so I asked David Parkes if it could be done. He said yes. Sandra still had no clue.

At the opening meeting that first morning, sure enough the Yellow Hall was half full. I was sitting in front of Mark's family group hoping all would go well. And when the meeting was over, David announced we were not done and said, 'I would like to invite Damien up here as I believe he has something to say to Sandra!' Up Damien went, as I turned to watch Sandra who said, 'Why is Damien going up there?' Damien, in front of all those people, over the microphone, asked Sandra to marry him. She was dumbstruck and paralysed. While he stood and waited, we were all urging Sandra to go up and give him her answer. She eventually came to her sense, joined Damien, and accepted the ring with a big 'YES!' She told me afterwards it was what she always wanted. During that really joy-filled week, so many people who were at that opening meeting stopped the couple in the street to congratulate them and wish them well. They were married in 2011 and are still a happily married couple.

Chapter Nineteen

MY SURPRISE 2014

One of the greatest surprises I myself could ever receive regarding Medjugorje came my way when, in early January 2014, my son Tony told me his wife Marian, who had been with Agnes and I on that first visit in 1997, wanted to return to Medjugorje with me in September. Marian had been to Medjugorje once more in 2001 with my granddaughter Sorcha but not since.

The fact that she wanted to return again was a pleasant surprise but not the real surprise. That came when I asked Tony, 'Does she want a single room or will she share?' and he responded, 'She will share - as I am going with her'.

That was a surprise, maybe a certain amount of shock and disbelief at first, but certainly joy. It was always a dream of mine that my family would experience Medjugorje but they never really showed any interest - and I wouldn't push. I knew if Our Lady wanted them there, She would get them there.

I was very excited and thankful that my son would be joining us that year. But then began to wonder what it would actually be like. What would he think of me and this work I was doing when he actually saw me doing it? Would he laugh? How would he get on with the group (a lot of whom would be older than him)? I was so pleased he was coming, but I was also nervous.

I needn't have worried. From the moment I introduced him to them at Dublin Airport they were great with him and he with them. Some he would have known already as they were my neighbours. He has an easy personality with people and was always there to help the older pilgrims in the group.

That trip happened to be my hundredth group; I had not said anything to Tony or Marian about this although most of the regular group would have known that this particular week was special to me.

What I did not know was behind the scenes arrangements were being made to celebrate the occasion. So one evening in Tomato House Restaurant the whole group gathered; along with Zelka and her husband from PIMK House where we were staying, Rosa from Tomato House where we had stayed for many years, and some of the locals with whom I had made friends over the years. The Marian Pilgrimage team were also there, David, Danijela, Mojca and Ozana. It was a very special evening and a memory to cherish.

There were greetings from Marian Pilgrimages in Dublin. There were gifts and bouquets of flowers. I didn't know what to do with the flowers as we were leaving the following day, and again it was Tony who surprised me by saying, 'When we are done here let's go down to Fr Slavko's grave and leave the flowers there.' I thought that was a great idea.

As the evening wore on Tony turned to me at one point and said, 'Mam, do you realise the reason you are here and the reason I am here is Dad's wish to come to Medjugorje.' It really came home to me at that moment how important keeping that promise to Bill had been.

On the way home that night Tony, Marian, myself and Joan walked down to Fr Slavko's grave and left the flowers. It was a beautiful, warm and calm evening. There was nobody there but ourselves, and we prayed quietly for a while and said goodbye to Fr Slavko for another year.

Tony really took to Medjugorje and has returned on a few occasions since. God willing, he will return this year with Marian to help in any way he can. He has said that is what he intends to do: help. September 2014 was a week to remember, but the greatest gift the Lord and His Blessed Mother could have granted me was the surprise presence of my son that year, which I am very thankful for.

Chapter Twenty

ALBERT'S STORY

One of the greatest blessings Medjugorje is known for is the confessions. There are so many confession boxes - twenty five on the left side of the church and about the same on the right side of the church - and it's still not enough. Go around the church any evening while the prayer programme is on and you will see queues outside every confession box, and many priests of so many languages seated along the outside walls of the church of St James. Two chairs, one for the priest, one for the penitent, and on the ground the card stating the language or languages of the confessor. It is extraordinary to see the number wanting to avail of this sacrament. Pope St. John Paul II once called Medjugorje, 'The confessional of the world' and it is certainly that! If, and when, you go to confession here, you need to be prepared to wait and wait and wait. Many come away from the sacrament crying, extremely emotional, but joyful, having reconciled, maybe after many years, with their Lord. I have been privileged to see so many instances of this - some in my own groups. One such story is Albert's - a story again of how our plans and the Lords plan may not always be in sync.

Mark, my reluctant pilgrim of 2009 who did became a regular, is a gardener. He works in a public park and he sees many people who use the park on a daily basis; joggers, walkers, families and dog walkers. Many are regulars, in the park every day, and because they are regulars, they would pass the time of day with Mark and eventually begin to chat with him.

Albert walked his dog, Snowy, in the park every day without fail. As Mark got to know him, he realised Albert lived alone and had many problems. Mark became a listening ear for Albert.

As Mark took a week away every year in September to visit Medjugorje, Albert always enquired on his return how Mark had got on or enjoyed himself and Mark would tell him what the week was like. Then out of the blue about April/May 2016 Mark informed me, 'Albert wants to go to Medjugorje'. Albert, who had not been to church or confession for over fifty years, wanted to go to Medjugorje.

Albert accompanied Mark in September 2016, having no clue what to expect. He got on well with the group and did what he could of the programme. He was in his seventies and climbing was certainly out, as his general health was not the best. One evening Mark mentioned to Albert he was going to confession. Albert wanted to go for a drink but decided he would accompany Mark, wait for him, and go for a drink later. It was quite late in the evening and on reaching the church grounds, they found only one English speaking priest still hearing confessions – and of course there was a queue. Mark decided to wait and Albert waited with him. Then Albert said to Mark, 'I think I will go to confession myself". To Mark this was something special.

However, as time went on, the queue moved very slowly. Albery was getting very nervous and was on the verge of changing his mind. Suddenly the priest came out of box and Mark, fearing he was leaving and not wanting Albert to miss the opportunity, ran up and asked the priest if he was leaving. The priest responded he had just come out for a smoke to which Mark replied, 'Oh good because I have a friend here who hasn't been to confession for over fifty years and is getting so nervous I'm afraid he won't wait.'

The priest immediately stubbed out the cigarette, went to where Albert still stood on the queue, took him by the arm and told him, 'I'm hearing your confession next' and led him to the confession box, to the dismay of the other people in the queue. When

Albert, after some time, emerged from the confession box he was at peace and content.

He continued to walk his dog in the park, chatting to Mark every day, but during 2017 his health deteriorated. His visits to the park stopped and in January 2018, sixteen months after his one and only visit to Medjugorje, Albert passed away. Maybe had he lived longer he might have returned to Medjugorje but it really didn't matter, for on the one visit he did make he was granted the grace to reconcile with his Lord.

Chapter Twenty-One

DAVID PARKES' STORY

David Parkes, as he tells his story, was a reluctant pilgrim to Medjugorje in 1989. He had two very special gifts. He excelled at football, which he loved, and he could sing very well. He originally chose football as his career and played professional football for Ireland. All went well with this career until 1977 when he was diagnosed with Crohn's disease. He then turned to singing, at which he was again very successful. He sang with his own band for fourteen years in the Burlington Hotel in Dublin.

However, this awful disease did not let up and resulted in a series of debilitating operations. After the last operation in 1989 the doctors told David there was nothing more they could do and gave him about fourteen weeks to live. He had to give up singing as his health deteriorated. With a young family to raise, things were not easy. Finances became stretched as he was not earning an income. There were three young children and a mortgage – debts were mounting.

It was then that his friends in the music world decided to hold a benefit night for him, and this was the night everything would change - though nobody knew that then, except the One, I believe, who set it all in motion.

There were many important people from the music industry, mostly friends of David's who were there to do their best for him that night. But the people who would eventually turn out to be the most important attendees were the Medjugorje people. The people who would approach and offer himself and Anne two free tickets to Medjugorje, this holy place.

David, who had been away from God and the church for eight years, admits he was sceptical. He could not know then he was actually being offered a ticket to the rest of his life. He chose to accept when he realised Medjugorje was only a few hours from Cavtat where he and Anne had spent their honeymoon.

By the time he and Anne were travelling, David (according to his doctors) had about two weeks to live. He was literally ravaged by this disease and getting worse as each day passed. Medjugorje was not where he wanted to be but he went because he thought it would be his last holiday with Anne. Fr Peter Rookey, the great healing priest, was spiritual director in their group, and David had a run-in with him at the airport.

David was not a happy man.

One day Fr Rookey was holding a healing service in the graveyard behind the church and Anne persuaded David to allow Fr Rookey to pray over him, promising if he did, they would leave Medjugorje and go to Cavtat for the rest of the time. He allowed Fr Rookey to pray with him. He rested in the spirit, rising after some time to realise he was standing straight, all the awful symptoms of this terrible disease were gone; sickness, vomiting, weakness, gone. He was healed.

However, it was two days later he was to receive the second and the most important healing of all – the spiritual one. David and Anne climbed Apparition Hill with a few others in the middle of the night. It was there, looking down on the lights of the valley below, that, having been away from the church for so long, he made peace with himself, with God and with his wife Anne. Up on Apparition Hill that night for the first time in a great many years, David sang the 'Ave Maria'.

This all happened, as he says himself, through the prayers of others. It all happened on that night of the benefit when he accepted the ticket to the rest of his life. In doing so he also accepted God's plan, for we know now, football and the secular music would come to mean nothing to him. He gave it all up to do the Lord's work. The rock and roll and pop songs were replaced by Christian music and he has travelled the world telling his story. His 'Evenings of Prayer Through Song' touches so many lives, giving hope where maybe hope was gone. May the Lord continue to bless him, his family and his endeavours.

Chapter Twenty-Two

WHAT SHE ASKS

I cannot finish this book without reflecting on what the Blessed Mother asks of us, and her reason for still appearing in Medjugorje after almost forty years.

Sometimes it is really hard to understand the wonder of the fact that, at 6.40pm in summertime and 5.40pm in wintertime, in a little village so far away from my home in Ireland, Heaven actually touches earth. So why does she come and what does she ask?

She comes to bring us back to her Son. Because of her love for us, to help us in any way she can to achieve this end. In the early days speaking to the visionaries, and through them to all of us, she set out the way to her Son saying, 'I give you five stones to beat your Goliath'.

First stone: Mass and the Eucharist

She made it clear to the children in the beginning how much more important it was to attend Mass rather than going to see her in apparition. Naturally to the children, seeing her every day had become the highlight of their day.

However, she explained to them that in the Mass they were in the presence of her Son, without whom she could do nothing. She also explained that in receiving the Eucharist they received the body of her Son, the food for their souls.

Second stone: Monthly confession

She invites us to go to monthly confession, for it is in this sacrament alone we get to reconcile with the Lord through his shepherd, the priest, especially if we are in a state of serious sin.

I know that when I go to confession there is no greater feeling upon receiving absolution, than the knowledge that all is right between me and the Lord. For a while anyway, for I am only a sinner, and always a sinner. Even if we are not in a state of serious sin, getting into the habit of monthly confession is a very good thing and always good for our souls.

Third Stone: The Rosary

'Always carry a rosary to show Satan you belong to me'. Again, this is what she invites us to do. One thing Our Lady never does is order or try to compel anyone to do anything, but because of her love for each of us she does invite us to take her advice. Our

Lady acknowledges our free will, but wants to help us on the path leading to her Son.

I have heard so many people say how boring the rosary is, that it is repetitive, all about Mary. Yes, it is repetitive, but if we really think about what it is telling us it is certainly not boring. If we really contemplate the rosary as we go along, it becomes, after all, the greatest story ever told. It is the story from beginning to end, of the Annunciation, Birth, Public Life, Passion, Death, and Resurrection of our Lord Jesus. If we remember, and use our God-given Imagination, travel with Mary his mother through his life, visualising what she has seen and heard, we will realise why she loves the rosary so much. She loves the rosary not because it's about her. She loves it because it is the story of her Son.

Fourth stone: Fasting

Our lady in Medjugorje asks those who can to fast on bread and water on Wednesdays and Fridays. For those who, for any reason cannot do this fast, she asks them to fast instead from something they really like. Maybe they could fast from television or sweets, etc. She stresses the importance of fasting and stated at one time that, 'Fasting can even stop wars'. I remember in the days when Mirjana met the groups and answered questions, she was asked, 'Is it okay to have coffee with bread instead of water' and she replied quite briefly, 'Our Lady says bread and water?'. Our Lady is not hard, and again it's an invitation, not an order – it is only asked of those who can do it.

Fifth Stone: Read the Bible every day.
The last stone she gives us is reading the bible every day, reading a little of the Word of God. She never said it had to be a lot but even a small piece, maybe pray a little beforehand, asking the Lord to help you understand the piece you choose to read. Reflect on that piece from time to time during the day. It is also important if you have a bible, to treat it with respect. Do not keep it in an attic with all the stuff you don't need, or in a drawer you never open, or on a shelf where it gathers dust. If you do have a bible it should never be closed but always open and if you have a stand especially for it all the better. 'The bible' Ivan once said, 'is not just for dusting. It should be kept in a visible place for everyone to see.'

When the young David in scripture met the giant Goliath, he knew he would probably die. After all, what did he have to fight with; a slingshot and a stone. Goliath could kill him with one blow of his hand, but David had the one thing Goliath did not. He had the Lord on his side. When that very young boy let fly that stone with his little slingshot, it hit the giant Goliath in the forehead and he dropped to the ground dead. So keep in mind the five stones given to us by the Blessed Mother, and if we choose to follow them, we are on the right track.

The following is a welcome contribution from one of my many Spiritual Directors.

MEDJUGORJE – A PRIEST'S EXPERIENCE AND REFLECTION ON THE SACRAMENT OF RECONCILIATION

I made my first pilgrimage to Medjugorje in 1985 after my first year in Seminary. At that time confessions were heard by priests sitting on chairs by the wall of the Church. On my second visit to Medjugorje in 2000 as a Priest, the physical structures in the village and Church grounds had changed, but the practice by priests of hearing confessions while sitting by the wall of the Church and now in the Confessionals had not changed. While I too receive the Sacrament of Reconciliation, I now could celebrate the Sacrament with pilgrims and be a minister of God's forgiveness.

Our Lady speaks of the five stones at the heart of the Christian journey, one being

Monthly Confession. It's a stone, not like that in the hands of those ready to stone the adulterous woman in the Gospel, but a stone symbolising the ripple effect of God's unconditional love and forgiveness. When pilgrims come to confession they are not facing the crowd ready to stone them but Jesus who is ready to say, 'Has no one condemned you? Go and sin no more.'

We are taught that we meet Jesus in a personal way in the Sacraments and that the Priest acts in the person of Christ. While hearing confessions in Medjugorje in 2001 I was led to use the Book of the Gospels in order for the penitent to meet Jesus personally. After the confession of sins and some spiritual guidance, I asked the penitent to allow the Holy Spirit to give them a page number of the Gospels in my personal bible - p5 - p153. After a moment of quiet, the person would give me the page number, and finding that page we spoke for a little while about how Jesus blessed the penitent with His living Word. Every time there was some some word, sentence, or even a story on that page which spoke directly to the person's life situation and struggle.

Jesus' words 'There is more joy in Heaven over one repentant sinner, than ninety nine virtuous people who have no need of forgiveness', are so important as I and every priest meet the sinner in Medjugorje and minister the forgiveness of God, the Merciful Father who is waiting for the sinner to return, to each unique person loved unconditionally by God. We can imagine how Our Lady, Our Mother, from the time of Jesus' death on Calvary, rejoices to see her children experience the joy of the Sacrament of Reconciliation. How the Sacrament of Reconciliation brings healing and joy to the sinner and many people who make the journey to Medjugorje burdened by sin, sadness and slavery return home with joy in their hearts, freedom in their spirit and a deep desire to live in goodness.

This one stone, Monthly Confession, is a gift to all of us on the journey of being and becoming the person God created us to be - called to use our gifts and talents in our relationship with God, neighbour and self. Jesus said that he came to call sinners - and confession is the Divine instrument to heal us and strengthen us.

It's a privilege to be a Minister of God's Forgiveness as a Priest in Medjugorje and to receive it as a Pilgrim.

Chapter Twenty-Three

MARIAN PILGRIMAGE TEAM IN MEDJUGORJE

When I went to Medjugorje first on pilgrimage in 1997 Philip Ryan worked for Marian Pilgrimages there. That first time I remember Claudia and Jozo were our guides. Nothing was too much trouble for them. Jozo told how, as a twelve year old boy, he was an eyewitness on the second day of the apparitions, how he watched Jakov Colo fly up the hill so fast that he, the fastest runner in the village at that time, couldn't catch him.

My first group in 1998, as far as I can remember, Philip was there again and Jozo, Ozana and Mojca were the guides. I remember Mojca specifically as, after breaking my wrist on Apparition Hill, she accompanied Philip when he took me to the hospital.

After 1998 Danijela joined the guides, who at that time alternated and included Mojca, Ozana and Vladka, (who loved jokes and later became a doctor).

Then over the years Marija, Tea, Tania, Danijela (two), have served us well.

David Parkes started work in Medjugorje in 2001. Since then, while some guides have move on to other things, the main guides today are still Danijela, Mojca, Ozana, Danijela (two), Tanja and Claudia.

While all of us pilgrims have grown older over the years, these guides, who were so young when we started, have matured with us. Just as we have come to know them really well, they have come to know us really well and have become good friends to so many of us.

When I think of the word "guides" I think of someone who brings people around museums and places of interest. They work mostly a set number of hours each day, and when the day is done, completely forget the people they meet on any specific day. It's just a job. Not so with the girls who work in Medjugorje for Marian Pilgrimages.

The Marian Pilgrimage season in Medjugorje in a long one, stretching from Easter to the end of October/early November every year. Once the season begins, David and these girls start working. Twenty-four hours a day seven days a week, they are working and always on call. They are with the pilgrims for early morning climbs. They don't just climb once in the week like the pilgrims do. They climb two or three times with different groups. We have opening and closing meetings, also a few times a week as groups come and go on different days.

They take us to Cenacolo (drug centre), Mother's Village, Blue Cross, and other places of interest. They come to the houses during the evening meal with the programme for the following day, to talk to the pilgrims and listen to our problems. Most of all, they are on-call through the night for anyone hurt or ill. Their help is so necessary in situations where pilgrims need to be hospitalised for any reason - as language and cultural differences can prove difficult.

I myself am so appreciative of the time David and the team in Medjugorje have been there for me personally, and for members of my groups, in times of difficulty.

Their care and kindness is beyond question. Through all the years and many problems they have never failed to meet our needs. They also have a great sense of fun and many joyful and laughter-filled moments have been spent in their company.

To me the title "guides" is not enough, for they are also prayerful and Spiritual. Because they bring so much of this dimension into their work I feel they are actually our "Spiritual Angels".

In writing this I would like to extend my thanks and the thanks of all my groups to David Parkes and these Angels for their care and attention over the years.

The houses

None of us could function in Medjugorje without accommodation. At this point I need to mention the houses we stay in. Tomato House hosted by Rosa and Franjo, RIP, were always kind and welcoming and supportive of all our pilgrims. Unfortunately as our pilgrims got older the lack of ground floor rooms and the absence of a lift forced us to move houses. So from 2001 to the present, we stay in the "PIMK" house and have been made very welcome by Zelka, her husband, and her family who also have been very kind to us.

Both houses have been exceptionally kind and helpful whenever a group member was sick or confined to their room. For all these years of service on behalf of myself and the groups I bring, I thank them. I must mention Mate and Monica in the Tomato restaurant who have always made me welcome. I have watched Mate mature from a teenager to a family man and a very successful businessman. I would also like to thank the various waiters, too many to mention, over the years who have always been welcoming and helpful to me and my groups. They helped me with my Croatian and I helped them with their English!

Chapter Twenty-Four

MARIAN PILGRIMAGES STORY

When I decided, at the instigation of others to use the "lockdown" to endeavour to write about my Medjugorje experiences and memories, I had a fair idea of the stories I wanted to relate. Then one day a thought came to me, 'What about Marian Pilgrimages itself?' I'm sure there has to be a story there.

Those of us who deal with Marian Pilgrimages on a regular basis know Tom Field. He is very much the public face of this company. He is at the airports (Dublin and regional) early mornings, evenings, whatever time we are travelling, seeing us off, dealing with last minute problems, etc. He's always the gentleman, always willing to help.

I do not want to forget the other Tom, Tom Glynn, who worked behind the scenes keeping everything on track. As I got to know him, I realised what a special person he really was. Lord rest him, he passed away in April 2013. Although he was in the background, he still played a huge part in forming the company that has become the Marian Pilgrimages of today. He had a heart of gold, in his quiet way helping where he felt help was needed, he had a great sense of humour and an ability to know how one's mind worked. He certainly knew how my mind worked. He was a generous and kind man.

So the thought came to me, 'How did the Marian Pilgrimages company start? How did the two Toms get together and form a company, which in the late 80's and through the 90's concentrated on Medjugorje?' I already knew snippets but felt there was more to the story, so I asked Tom Field, who confirmed I was right. There is a story and a great story.

I met with Tom and this is the story in his words and how he tells it.

'I first heard of Medjugorje in 1986 when myself and two friends drove to Waterford, to hear a priest called Fr Donal O'Callaghan speak of it. Fr Donal has since passed away (RIP). I was amazed at his speech and what he had to say about Medjugorje and what was happening there. On my return I talked to others in Top Flight (my place of employment), as more and more people were asking about Medjugorje. It was very difficult to get there at that time as it involved going half way around Europe and it was also very expensive.

'Myself and other interested parties had a meeting in Dublin to put our thoughts and ideas together. Top Flight got slightly involved that first year. It was the mid 80's and still hard to get to Medjugorje.

'My friend Tom Glynn travelled abroad yearly with his wife Maria and on one of these occasions he went to Yugoslavia. This was before the breakdown of communism and the start of the civil war. Tom worked with Club Travel, and I with Top Flight. They were two arms of the same company - Club Travel was the holiday section and Top Flight covered the pilgrimage section in which I worked.

'When Tom was on holidays he did not like to just sit in the sun. He liked to drive. While in the former Yugoslavia, he was driving down a mountain road in Bosnia when he saw what he thought was an airport, so he checked it out.

'Talking to myself and a few others on his return he said "You know that place you talk of - Medjugorje? Well there is a local military airport close by and they take commercial flights. It's only twenty five minutes from the village." We realised this would be more convenient as flying into Dubrovnik or Split meant a long bus journey to Medjugorje.

'It was about then Club Travel had decided to buy an aircraft of its own. They eventually purchased, from the USA, a Boeing 727 jet, which was brought to

Ireland. From there everything started. An American pilot called Fred was employed to fly the plane.

'We were getting enquiries from all over Ireland as interest in Medjugorje grew and this interest showed no sign of slowing down. As interest continued to grow, we held a seminar in Dublin city centre, invited people to come and talk about Medjugorje and they did come from all over the country. The interest became huge. We had four group leaders, who all separately wanted to bring groups to Medjugorje.

'We questioned: "Why not use the newly purchased aircraft, which was bringing holidaymakers everywhere, and fly it to Mostar?" So Fred, the chief pilot, flew to Bosnia to check the airport as regards takeoffs and landings.

'The name of the plane was "Queen of Peace" even though it was only being used for holidaymakers. This was 1986.

'In that same year we had a weekend convention in Renvyle House. It was made up mainly of group leaders from San Giovanni and Medjugorje and over a thousand people attended. We had invited Fr Slavko to attend and to speak about Medjugorje. Interest continued to grow.

'At the seminar someone asked Fr Slavko, "What about these commercial companies mixing spiritual and commercial, are they only in it for the money?" Fr

Slavko cut them short saying "These companies have to exist if you want to get to Medjugorje. It would be ideal if a happy balance could be kept between the commercial and spiritual."

'Flights to Mostar started and on one of these flights Fred (with whom I had become quite friendly) asked me to come up to the cockpit as we approached Mostar to point out the huge cross everyone was talking about. He promised that in future he would try to point it out to the pilgrims on approach to the airport.

'We boarded buses for Medjugorje, with guides Donnacha and Graham. The procedure was different then to what it would become and is today. We had used an agent to book the houses in advance for us, as we thought, but the Americans were coming with their dollars up front, going directly to the houses who were of course accepting the dollars. As a result of this when we arrived there might be room for two in one house, three in another, and so on. It took a lot of time dropping people off at different houses but no-one complained.

'Also, there was only one communal toilet in each house, but again nobody complained. The numbers for Medjugorje continued to grow. Club Travel as it was then closed in 1989 and with its closure went the plane. The people from Top Flight still stayed loyal and remained involved in Medjugorje. As a result of this I mentioned to Tom Glynn on one occasion that I felt that there was an opening here. Also because of Club Travel closing, it became necessary for us to buy seats from two different companies. Some group leaders (some still alive today), suggested we start a company.

'Having thought about it, Tom Glynn and myself decided to do this but we didn't have a name for the company.

'At that time we worked out of Abbey Mall in Middle Abbey Street and one day a priest came in to book a small group to Medjugorje. I asked him if he could think of a name for the company. He said he would and left. The priest came back in minutes and said, "I have it, Marian Pilgrimages." The priest was Fr Cecil Johnson (still with us) and I responded, "That's the name".

'In 1991 we moved from Abbey Mall to 25 Eden Quay. We were still buying tickets from two other companies and even though there were other tour operators going to Medjugorje, we had more pilgrims on the first flights to Medjugorje that year before the war started than the tour operators. Those pilgrims had remained loyal to us, and have done to this day. Medjugorje was our only destination then.

'That same year trouble was brewing in former Yugoslavia and there was outbreaks of war in parts of

Croatia called Oziek and Vukovar. It started gradually and people were getting nervous.

'One day Liam Prendergast, one of our group leaders, came into the office. Liam was also, at that time, head of the Medjugorje Council of Ireland. He came to me asking for my help. Liam had been a Major General with the Irish Army and had served in the Congo among other places. He was involved in helping the people of Medjugorje and that region during the war.

'He told me that he had 10,000 sterling and 180kg of medical supplies and needed my help to get them to Medjugorje for the people who were being badly affected by the war.

'I said I would help in any way I could, and as I had Marian Pilgrimage business to attend to in Medjugorje, I decided to accompany Liam on his mission.

'We flew to London Heathrow, where we would get connecting flights to Belgrade and Sarajevo. Before we could board the plane, we had to pay £20 war tax. Liam had the £10,000 in a leather belt around his waist. Medical supplies were on board the plane.

'I noticed a strange thing about that flight. There was not a single female on the aircraft. I realised they were all males, Croats, Muslim and Serbs travelling back to their home countries to fight each other in a war. They had lived so many years together under

Tito's Yugoslavia. It was sad. Fr Slavko was to meet us in Sarajevo the following day to take the supplies. Because of the weight we were carrying, Fr Anton from the monastery in Sarajevo met us. Fr Slavko in the meantime had sent word to the monastery that he couldn't get to Sarajevo. Travelling to the monastery from the airport we had the boot of the car open because of the supplies when I thought I heard gunshots. I asked Fr Anton about it but he said it was okay just Croatia and Bosnia celebrating the ratification of their independence so no need to worry.

'The following day Fr Slavko sent a message. He could not get past Mostar to come and collect us with the van. He said to stay where we were, and he would advise us what to do.

'That night all hell broke loose. The Serbs attacked the airport and twenty three people were killed. The same airport we flew into the day before - so we didn't really know if the gunfire we heard on arrival was actually a celebration or the start of the war.

'The Yugoslavian National Army, the JNA, had a huge base beside the monastery. Fr Anton assured us we were safe there. The local Serbs, because the priests had been good to them over the years, had given their word they would not touch the monastery. However, that night I was asleep when the gunfire started, by the Serb Militia literally outside the window. The seminarians in panic were running up and down the corridors. Between them they had one gun.

'I was sleeping in the room next to Liam and we were told to turn our lights off. Going into the corridor I noticed a light under Liam's door and knocked. When he answered I said, "Liam there's trouble outside". Because of his army experience he would be more used to this kind of situation than I would. He turned his light off. The seminarians were still running up and down the corridors with their one gun. Trying to calm them I asked, "What do you think you can do with one gun?" They were very afraid. Two days after that, the shelling came from the top of the mountain into the middle of Sarajevo - the Muslin section.

'There was no way we could use the normal means of getting home. The Serbs were now in charge of the airport. Liam wanted to get to meet the head of the UN contingent in Sarajevo who was a friend of his, hoping he could help. Fr Slavko had already sent word there was no way he could get to us. We just had to forget about it.

'The following day we headed to Sarajevo to meet Liam's friend. On the way we came to a checkpoint manned by civilians in makeshift uniforms carrying machine guns. They waved us through.

'In Sarajevo, Liam's friend arranged for us to fly to Belgrade the following day on a UN flight. Relieved, as we believed our return home was organised, we headed back to the monastery. However, coming to the same checkpoint this time we were stopped and questioned. Fr Anton was driving, and Liam was with him in the front of the car. I was in the back with Fr Johann. One of these guys put his gun to my head I just looked forward. After a while he took the gun down then put it back again to my cheek. I kept looking forward and eventually he put the gun down and walked back to his position. On arrival back to the monastery, Fr Johann asked if I had been afraid when the gun was against my head and I told him, "Yes very much so" and he responded, "You didn't show it".

'We saw a really good example of propaganda at that time. One day in the communal room in the monastery, we were watching local TV. It was relaying what was going on outside and what was happening with the seminarians. All you had to do was go to the window to see they had it right. Fr Anton getting up said "Let me show you something." Switching channels he turned on Belgrade TV and there on the screen was Karadic and Milosevic coming off a plane. Being interviewed they declared: "We are not the oppressors here, we are being attacked by these people." Yet looking out the window, we could see their guns at the top of the hill. They were telling the world they were not the oppressors and we were looking first-hand at the proof that they were. In the future they would both be tried and convicted of war crimes.

'The day after we left, the Serbs broke their promise to the priests and took over the monastery. They took away the priests and seminarians, eventually letting the seminarians go but keeping the priests. They took the medical supplies. Liam eventually got word that the cash had reached Medjugorje, but nobody knows how.

'As events unfolded, our flight to Belgrade did not materialise but we did get to join a French convoy going to the border. Liam had managed to get our names down for that.

'A Serbian girl had asked to join the convoy. She was going back to Belgrade and she was accepted. Liam and I were dressed in suits and ties, never realising this would prove a problem on this journey. At one stage we were pulled over to the side of the road. We didn't understand this. Being with the UN meant you were supposed to have complete freedom of movement.

'But these were local Serb Militia army with their guns, who did not recognise the UN, and they pulled us in. They questioned Liam and I, trying to make out that because of the way we were dressed, we were EU monitors, which was bad news for us because it was the EU who were responsible for giving Croatia and Bosnia their independence so we were in trouble.

'The Serbian girl got out of the car and approached the men questioning us. She told them who she was and they sent one of the soldiers to their commander in the local village. As a result we were allowed to return to the convoy and continue our journey. I believe that girl saved our lives that day.

'We had no contact with our families in days, no contact with anybody at home in Ireland, and they were very worried. Thank God we got home safely and that was the end of that part of the story.

'I went back to Medjugorje again later that year as once more I had Marian Pilgrimage business to do there. It was 1991 and the war was still going on and while we were aware of it, hearing gunfire in the distance and seeing the flashes of light, it was not actually in Medjugorje itself.

There were a few people in Medjugorje at that time but really very few. At this point I asked Tom, 'How did Marian Pilgrimages survive as Medjugorje was their only destination?'

He replied 'Tony Carroll RIP, a group leader, was coming into the office a few times a week and one day he said, "Tom why don't we do a pilgrimage to Fatima?" and we did.'

'We got 240 people for that trip. I travelled with them and we had a fantastic week. During the war years in Croatia/Bosnia we took some trips to Fatima and a few smaller pilgrimages to other places - nothing on the scale we had been doing in Medjugorje and they were very lean years.'

Asking about Tom Glynn and his role, Tom continued, 'Tom Glynn remained in Dublin keeping an eye on things there, and running everything while I travelled. We kept in touch all the time and things would never have run as smoothly as they did without Tom Glynn.

'This civil conflict would cause so much heartbreak and after many deaths and atrocities on all sides, finally this terrible war ended in 1995. People had already begun to return to Medjugorje on a small scale. I had gone back myself in the meantime, ensuring it was safe to travel. The guides in Medjugorje had been keeping us informed.

'The numbers increased again, and from then on, for a number of years, we put all our energies into Medjugorje. Philip Ryan had joined the local guides at that time and remained with us until he resigned at the end of 2000. David Parkes then joined the team in Medjugorje in 2001. The numbers continued to increase, and we have been so blessed with all of our pilgrims and guides through the years.

'We eventually decided to invite the guides to Ireland and that's when something new started. The pilgrims loved the guides and gave them a great welcome. We started bringing them every year to various venues which were hosted by different group leaders. The guides would speak in churches and each year as a result, the number of venues increases. Danijela, Mojca, Ozana and Danijela (two) have been regulars for a number of years.

'This year Tanja came as Danijela (two) was unable to. They travel with me, North, South, East and West and they bring Medjugorje to so many people who cannot get there.

'Even now they are working in Medjugorje doing Virtual Pilgrimages by means of social media.

'Over the years Marian Pilgrimages has expanded and I have met so many people and heard great stories. I so am glad that something Tom Glynn and I started so many years ago, has grown and continues to give joy to so many.'

At this point Tom's story ends and I continue.

Marian Pilgrimages has continued to go from strength to strength. In 1998 they moved from 25 Eden Quay to 19 Eden Quay, a much larger premises, and over the years have filled that premises with a very pleasant staff. Niall Glynn, son of Tom, is at the helm.

They do have a holiday section, Croatia Tours, and now not only do they still go to Medjugorje but also to all of the other pilgrim sites. From small acorns grow large oaks and no doubt the seed of Marian Pilgrimages was sown by Tom Field's visit to Fr Donal's talk. This resulted in his increased interest in Medjugorje.

When getting there seemed so difficult, Tom Glynn's drive down that Bosnian mountainside and spotting Mostar airport would change everything. These two friends, the two Toms, started something back then that so many of us have reaped the benefit of since.

Recalling Fr Slavko's response to the comment about commercial companies being in it only for the money, hearing Tom's story about the war years, the risks taken and the birth and growth of a company, confirms the feeling I had that the Marian Pilgrimage story is worth telling.

SUMMING UP

On the 19th of April 2020 I made a decision to use the "Lockdown" to write a book specifically about Medjugorje and some of the amazing people I've met, and also the joy being a Group Leader has brought me.

On the 20th of April I began to write and could not believe how easily the words came. Twenty three years worth of memories, experiences, life-changing stories flowed so quickly from brain to hand to page.

Apart from the personal stories told in the book, looking back, it is hard to believe how many mornings we rose at 6am, not to climb hills or mountains, but to stand at the bottom of the steps at Vicka's old house in Bijakovici to hear her speak at 8.30am. The same at Mirjana's house. I recall crisp October mornings, praying the rosary outside Mirjana's house very early waiting for her to speak at 8.30am. Not forgetting Jakov, we stood outside his house also, always hours before he was due to speak. Ivan and Marija, when they were in the village, spoke in the Yellow Hall. Ivanka rarely spoke in public. Wherever they were we queued, waited and enjoyed the experience.

Whenever there was a public apparition, usually at 10pm, we climbed early, 6.00pm, to get 'a good rock' to be as near the visionary as possible. Usually at the last minute dozens of people would come crowding up the hill and our view would be blocked anyway! Of course the Prayer programme, outdoor Adoration and talks all meant so much. Those weeks in Medjugorje were always busy weeks and while we came home exhausted, at the same time we came home renewed and refreshed.

At my age and in my state of health it is logical to believe my time for doing this work is drawing to a close. While my brain, thank God, continues to be very active and the ability to sit, listen and talk to the pilgrims has not diminished, my body, on the other hand, has fallen well behind.

Every time I have thought of or spoken of giving up for any particular reason, help comes to enable me to carry on. When I board that plane and arrive in Medjugorje I seem to always have the extra strength required to do what's needed to fulfil the promise made to the Blessed Virgin all those years ago. No doubt she sends the help.

For so many years I was independent. I travelled to

the airport alone; it was no problem waiting for that last pilgrim at check in, no problem lifting my own luggage. However, those years are gone and I am not too proud, though perhaps sad, to admit I cannot do these things alone anymore. However, there are stalwarts in the groups always willing to help.

In my May Groups for some years now, Joan has taken over looking after my luggage and been a great help in Medjugorje. I use the airport wheelchair facility instead of walking the long distance to Departures and I have realised I don't need to wait for the last pilgrim at check-in.

For the September Group, (always the largest) Mark the 'reluctant pilgrim' has been my stalwart at this time for a number of years. Joan, now retired, has begun to come at this time also.

I have to admit the greatest gift came my way in 2014 when my own son, Tony, expressed the wish to join the group and has done so fairly consistently ever since. He also has proved himself to be a support and a great help to me.

Addendum

DIVINE MERCY STORY

There is another story to tell, nothing to do with Medjugorje, but another story about Bill and it involves Divine Mercy.

In 2011 I wrote my life story for a project I was undertaking. Having related the story to Paul Wallace, he encouraged me to tell the story at the Medjugorje weekend in Knock in November. Being nervous about this, I brought a copy of the story to Medjugorje in October. I needed to run it by a few friends as a fore-runner to my Testimony at Knock.

As a result of this, David Parkes decided to record the story. The night we recorded the story, I couldn't sleep. I switched on the light at one stage and it was 3.00AM exactly. For some reason Divine Mercy came into my mind, so I lay down and started to say the Chaplet. Then something extraordinary happened.

It was like a loud voice in my head said, 'NO' and in succession came three thoughts as if someone was speaking them. Divine Mercy - Bill's confession - You forgot - and I knew the story was not done without the following:

Bill never missed mass but would not go to confession, so consequently would not receive the Eucharist. I prayed every day and said, 'Lord, let Bill receive the sacraments before he dies'. I prayed the Chaplet of Divine Mercy every day at 3pm.

I had the life story of Sr. Faustina (as she was then, before canonisation). Bill read this book and said to me: 'Is that story anything to do with that thing you do at three o'clock every day and if so, can I do it with you?'. So we did the Chaplet together every day, and in time followed it with the rosary (this was before Bill read about Medjugorje).

One Saturday afternoon he said to me, 'What time are confessions in our church this evening?' and I replied, '6.30pm'. After a slight pause he said, 'I think I'll go to confession this evening'. I said okay and in my mind thanked the Lord. He did go that night, for the first time in thirty three years. He received the Eucharist for two weekends and then stopped. When I asked why he replied, 'I don't feel I have been to confession as I didn't get enough penance for thirty three years', and there was no convincing him otherwise.

I was going on a weekend retreat in Avila which was given by a priest called Fr Ronnie Mitchell, RIP, in October 1996 and for the first time ever Bill decided to join me.

He loved it and decided to go to confession to Fr Ronnie. After spending an hour with Fr Ronnie, he said to me, 'Now, I've really been to confession, I am home'.

On leaving that weekend, Bill told Fr Ronnie we would be back for his next weekend in May 1997 and we booked before we left that day. However, that May weekend in 1997 was the weekend Bill was dying. He wanted so much to talk to Fr Ronnie that I called Avila and spoke to him. I explained the position to him and asked him to visit Bill if possible. The following day, Sunday the 11th of May, Fr Ronnie called to see Bill who was already on a morphine pump and not communicating. Fr Ronnie took his hand and said, 'Bill we were expecting you in Avila'. Bill's eyes flew open and he tried to sit up. Fr Ronnie calmed him and stayed with him for about thirty minutes. Bill died the following day, May 12th.

Fr Ronnie told me later that Bill had told him that my prayers had brought him to Avila and that I had a habit of leaving holy books around for him to read. When Bill decided to go to confession, as far as we knew he was in good health. We could not know only six months remained for him.

I also promoted the Divine Mercy at that time and it was only in Medjugorje in October, in a week without a group, I realised the significance of the two incidents as Jesus promises Divine Mercy to the dying.

A PRAYER

COMPOSED BY

Carmel Kelly

Lord Jesus how I love you
at the start of everyday
I praise and thank you for my life
and I promise not to stray.

And it always seems so easy
when there's only you and I,
just an extra little effort
nothing to do, but try.

But I'm just a humble sinner Lord
destined in this world to live.
Where taking is the expected thing
And it's considered odd to give.

And living in this material world,
its sad to have to say,
I've slipped and fallen many times,
by noon time every day.

But I thank you for your renewal Lord
Which has made me so aware.
That no natter how I slip and fall,
You are always there.

Through every hour of every day
Your home is firmly in my heart
And I know that in my sleeping
We are never far apart.

And as the night is coming on,
And to pray I once more kneel.
I thank you for the gift you've given,
To pen these words I feel

And just before I close my eyes,
There's one more thing to say.
For the wonderful gift of your
Precious love my Lord,
I thank you at the end of every day.

ACKNOWLEDGEMENTS

Please forgive me in advance for whoever I leave out for I just know I'll leave someone out.

Firstly to all who allowed me to tell their stories. For those who encouraged me. For Niall Glynn and Marian Pilgrimages for all their help and encouragement. For Joan who spent many hours typing my notes. For Antoinette who proofread the manuscript. To Fr Tom for all his advice and input. To Tom Field for his history of the early days of Marian Pilgrimages. Also at this point, I would like to extend my thanks to all the priests, too numerous to mention, who have joined my groups as spiritual directors over the years.

The writing of this book was made possible by the support of family and friends, who looked after my needs and saved me from distraction during this time, so my thanks to all.

POST SCRIPT

It is with great sadness that I have to write this postscript to say that Carmel received her heavenly wings on the 26th of Sept 2020.

I first met Carmel when myself and two friends were put into her group, without her knowing, in May 2000, and of course we were made welcome. From that time on I travelled with Carmel every year and sometimes twice a year. We became good friends and would meet regularly.

I was very blessed to have spent so much time with her during the lockdown. She would phone me every few days and read me her stories. She was really excited about her project and intended to go into Marian Pilgrimages and ask the staff to type it up.

As the chapters were adding up, I suggested that once the restrictions were lifted I would bring the laptop over to her house and transcribe her stories. So on the 9th of June I travelled over to her and we began. I made the trip twice a week and we worked together: she read her stories and I typed. Then I would come home and make all the corrections, which I would then send to my friend Antoinette to proofread for me.

This was really a miracle-work. She started writing on the 19th of April and we finished the first proof on the 19th of July.

After that she would make little changes. Right up to the time she went into hospital on the 1st of September she was making corrections to my typing. She was finally happy with the finished product and made me promise to make sure it was printed.

Carmel, as a young person, always wanted to write a book, and her Lord honoured her wish.

I will miss you greatly, Carmel! The first trip to Medjugorje after the Pandemic will certainly be different but I know you were ready and are now reunited with your husband Bill.

On behalf of all the pilgrims you brought in your 116 groups, thank you Carmel for always being there for your pilgrims and for listening to us and telling your stories. We were blessed to have you as our group leader.

God bless and rest in peace.

Joan